U0627917

中国职业教育发展报告

Report on the Development of Vocational Education in China

教育部职业教育发展中心　组编

Compiled by Center for Vocational Education Development

Ministry of Education, P.R. China

中国教育出版传媒集团
China Education Press & Media Group Ltd

高等教育出版社·北京
Higher Education Press　Beijing

图书在版编目（CIP）数据

中国职业教育发展报告：汉、英／教育部职业教育
发展中心组编 . -- 北京：高等教育出版社，2025. 1.
ISBN 978-7-04-064168-4

I . G719.2

中国国家版本馆 CIP 数据核字第 20244CV622 号

Zhongguo Zhiye Jiaoyu Fazhan Baogao

| 策划编辑 | 贾瑞武　王素霞 | 责任编辑 | 于　腾 | 封面设计 | 李树龙 |
| 版式设计 | 李树龙 | 责任校对 | 高　歌 | 责任印制 | 赵义民 |

出版发行	高等教育出版社	网　　址	http://www.hep.edu.cn
社　　址	北京市西城区德外大街4号		http://www.hep.com.cn
邮政编码	100120	网上订购	http://www.hepmall.com.cn
印　　刷	北京盛通印刷股份有限公司		http://www.hepmall.com
开　　本	787mm×1092mm 1/16		http://www.hepmall.cn
印　　张	9		
字　　数	130 千字	版　　次	2025 年 1 月第 1 版
购书热线	010-58581118	印　　次	2025 年 1 月第 1 次印刷
咨询电话	400-810-0598	定　　价	32.00 元

本书如有缺页、倒页、脱页等质量问题，请到所购图书销售部门联系调换
版权所有　侵权必究
物 料 号　64168-00

目　录

Table of Contents

Chapter Two: Valuable Experience   / 102

Chapter Three: Strategic Tasks   / 114

前　言

中国职业教育发展源远流长，曾在世界文明史和教育史上留下浓墨重彩。进入新时代，面对经济、社会、人口、环境、就业等多方面挑战和机遇，中国加快发展现代职业教育，在有效支撑国家经济社会高质量发展、不断满足人民群众对美好生活的追求、持续支持学生多样化成长成才、积极服务构建全面开放新格局等方面取得了历史性成就。中国职业教育无论是外延还是内涵、广度还是深度、规模还是质量，都发生了史无前例和鼓舞人心的变革。

2023年，中国高中阶段教育毛入学率91.80%，其中中等职业教育在校生占高中阶段教育总数近40%，助力基础教育普及水平总体达到世界中上行列；高等职业教育年招生数超过普通本科，助力高等教育毛入学率突破60%，实现历史性跨越，推动高等教育进入世界公认的普及化阶段。这不仅是职业教育在中国教育改革发展大潮中的亮点，也对世界职业教育发展进程具有重要意义。

中国以发展职业教育服务国家发展、传承中华文明、弘扬工匠精神，持续推进产教深度融合、校企有效合作，支持构建技能型社会，建成世界上规模最大的现代职业教育体系，形成了政府主导、学校主体、产教融合的职教发展模式，为技能人才公平成长、终身发展撑起重要舞台。职业教育成为支持中国成为制造大国、迈向制造强国的重要力量。

当今世界正经历百年未有之大变局，不稳定性不确定性明显增加。应对世界之变、时代之变、格局之变，适应科技革命、数字革命、产业变革新挑战，需要把加快发展现代职业教育摆在更加突出的位置，纳入全球发展总体部署，促进职业教育与经济社会同步发展，为产业经济与服务市场提供坚实的技能人才支撑。当前，中国已经步入进一步全面深化改革、推进中国式现代化建设的崭新阶段，将统筹推进教育科技人才一体化发展，致力于在2035年建成教育强国。中国愿以职业教育赋能人类命运共同体建设，与世界各国携手并进，以更加开放的理念、更加开放的标准、更加开放的资源、更加开放的机制，共同探索职业教育发展的新路径、新模式，共同应对全球发展面临的挑战，增进人民福祉，促进全球可持续发展。

《中国职业教育发展报告》用大量事实、数据和案例，从发展成就、基本经验、战略任务、主要举措四个方面，全景式呈现了2012年以来中国职业教育在制度构建、体系完善、产教融合、质量提升、国际合作等方面的实践经验和创新成果，展现了中国职业教育发展的蓬勃生机与强劲动力，以前瞻性视角描绘了中国职业教育在新时代背景下的发展蓝图和战略任务，为未来中国职业教育的持续繁荣与全球职业教育事业的共同发展提供参考与启示。

第一编　发展成就

中国高度重视发展职业教育，把职业教育作为国民教育体系和人力资源开发的重要组成部分，赋予职业教育培养多样化人才、传承技能、促进就业创业的重要职责。2012年以来，中国职业教育在规模、体系、模式、质量、国际交流合作等方面取得了历史性成就，发生了格局性变化，成为培养高技能人才、能工巧匠、大国工匠的主阵地。

一、建成世界规模最大的职业教育体系

政府统筹整合社会各界力量，职普融通、育训并举，逐步建立起适应经济社会发展、服务全民终身学习的职业教育体系。职业学校每年培养毕业生超过1,000万名、开展职业培训约1,300万人次。现代制造业、战略性新兴产业和现代服务业等领域，一线新增从业人员70%以上来自职业学校。

（一）形成结构完善的培养体系

1. 职业学校层级完整，成为技能人才供给的主渠道

形成"中等职业教育—高等职业教育（专科）—高等职业教育（本科）"的层级结构。高等职业教育（专科）的主体地位不断增强，高等职业教育（本

科）稳步发展（图1-1）。

2023年，共有职业学校11,133所，其中中等职业学校（简称"中职"）9,553所[1]，高等职业学校（专科）（简称"高职专科"）1,547所，高等职业学校（本科）（简称"高职本科"）33所。2012年以来，呈现中等职业学校数量缓慢减少，高等职业学校数量稳步增长的发展态势（图1-2）。

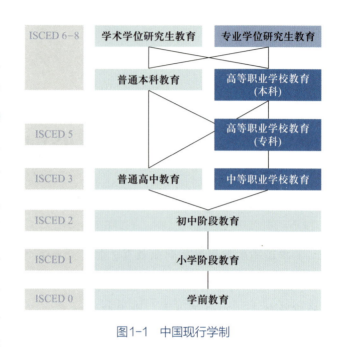

图1-1　中国现行学制

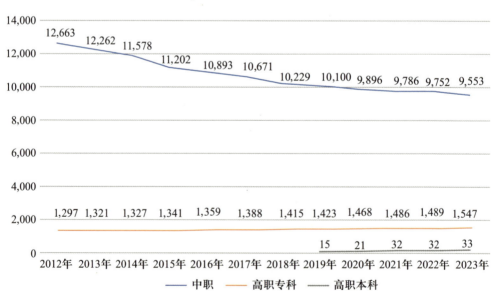

图1-2　2012—2023年职业学校数量变化（单位：所）[2]

1　含技工院校。

2　数据来源：全国教育事业发展统计公报（2012年—2023年）；人力资源和社会保障事业发展统计公报（2012年—2023年）。

职业学校毕业生成为城镇新增劳动力和一流产业技术工人的重要来源。2023年，职业学校在校生3,478.28万人，其中，中等职业学校1,737.96万人、高等职业学校（含高职本科）1,740.32万人（图1-3）。2022年职业学校毕业生突破1,000万人，2023年达到1,094万人（图1-4）。新增城镇就业人口中，高等职业学校毕业生占比稳步增加，2020年突破30%，2022年突破40%，2023年达到44.77%（图1-5）。

职业学校教师数量稳步增长，结构进一步优化。职业学校专任教师总数从2012年的130.44万人逐年增加到2023年的145.02万人（图1-6）；兼职教师队伍不断扩大，2023年达到25.37万人，较上一年增加9.40%。其中大国工匠、劳动模范超过8,000人，行业导师承担的年课时总量达4.28亿学时。

2. 职业教育内部纵向贯通，与普通教育横向融通

职业教育内部以及职业教育与普通高等教育的衔接通道为学生发展提供更多选择。2014年起，中国将高职考试招生与普通高考相对分开，以省为主探

图1-3　2012—2023年职业教育在校生数变化（单位：万人）[1]

1　数据来源：全国教育事业发展统计公报（2012年—2023年）；人力资源和社会保障事业发展统计公报（2012年—2023年）。

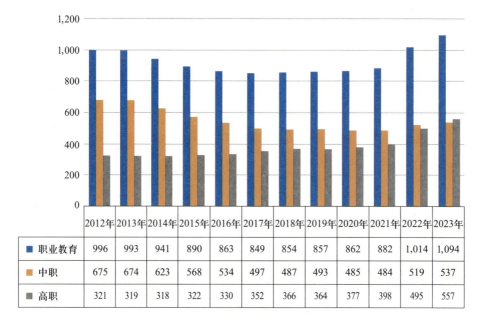

图1-4　2012—2023年职业教育毕业生数变化（单位：万人）[1]

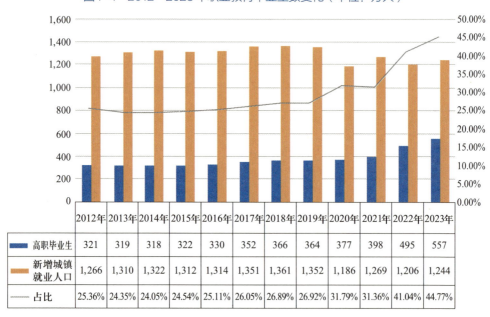

图1-5　2012—2023年高职（含高职本科）毕业生和新增城镇就业人口规模及占比变化（单位：万人）[2]

1　数据来源：全国教育事业发展统计公报（2012年—2023年）；人力资源和社会保障事业发展统计公报（2012年—2023年）。

2　数据来源：全国教育事业发展统计公报（2012年—2023年）；人力资源和社会保障事业发展统计公报（2012年—2023年）。

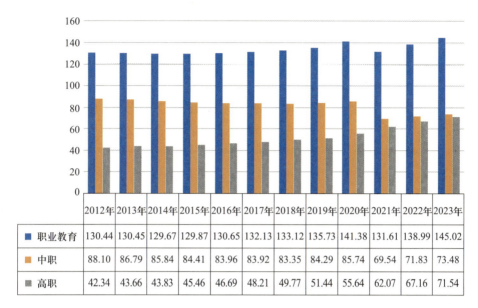

	2012年	2013年	2014年	2015年	2016年	2017年	2018年	2019年	2020年	2021年	2022年	2023年
■ 职业教育	130.44	130.45	129.67	129.87	130.65	132.13	133.12	135.73	141.38	131.61	138.99	145.02
■ 中职	88.10	86.79	85.84	84.41	83.96	83.92	83.35	84.29	85.74	69.54	71.83	73.48
■ 高职	42.34	43.66	43.83	45.46	46.69	48.21	49.77	51.44	55.64	62.07	67.16	71.54

图1-6　2012—2023年职业教育专任教师规模变化（单位：万人）[1]

索实施"文化素质+职业技能"评价方式。之后，高职分类考试招生规模逐年扩大，已经成为高职学校面向中职学校和普通高中招生的主渠道。此外，中高职五年一贯制、3年中职+2年高职、3年高职+2年本科等多种衔接培养方式为学生发展提供了不同选择，2023年仅五年一贯制由中职转入高职的学生就有60.70万人，占当年高职专科招生的10.94%[2]。每年约有20%的高职毕业生通过"专升本"考试[3]进入普通高等学校学习。

职业教育与普通教育渗透融合成效日显。近十年，全国有4,500余所职业学校支持近11万所中小学开展劳动教育实践和职业启蒙教育，引导青少年树立技能报国、技能成才理想，参与学生超过1,500万人。部分地方主动探索中职学校和普通高中教师互派、资源互通、课程互选、学分互认。

1　数据来源：全国教育事业发展统计公报（2012年—2023年）。2021年—2023年数据不含技工学校。

2　数据来源：2023年全国教育事业发展统计公报。

3　学生通过考试，由专科学校升入本科学校。此类考试由省级教育行政部门领导、各省教育考试院统一组织管理。考试选拔对象为全日制高职（专科）学校应届毕业生，通过"专升本"考试考入本科学校继续接受2–3年的全日制本科教育。

3. 学校教育与职业培训并重

推行终身职业技能培训制度。国家实施职业技能提升行动，支持职业学校开展补贴性培训，扩大面向职工、就业重点群体和贫困劳动力的培训规模，近五年政府补贴性培训年均近2,400万人次。教育部、中华全国总工会联合面向一线产业工人实施"求学圆梦行动"，累计帮助240余万名一线职工提升学历、1,000余万人次接受职业培训。

（二）形成统筹有力的管理体系

1. 构建系列法律制度

中国高度重视职业教育立法工作。国家层面，1996年颁布实施《中华人民共和国职业教育法》，标志职业教育发展进入法治化轨道，2022年完成职教法修订，固化了职业教育大发展20余年来的基本经验和制度成果。地方结合需要，有计划地制定地方职业教育条例、配套相应的执法检查制度，完善职业教育法律法规体系。2022年以来，安徽、天津、山东、四川等省和直辖市的职教条例已颁布施行，湖南、河南、辽宁、山西等省正面向社会征求意见，青岛、无锡、深圳、广州等城市已将制定或修订条例纳入立法规划。天津市颁布施行《天津市职业教育产教融合促进条例》，江苏、吉林、衢州、宁波、台州、伊犁哈萨克自治州等地出台了各自的校企合作促进条例。

2. 宏观管理分工明确

国务院统筹协调全国职业教育工作。教育部负责职业教育工作的统筹规划、综合协调、宏观管理。教育部、人力资源和社会保障部以及有关行业主管部门在国务院规定的职责范围内，分别负责有关的职业教育工作。教育部会同有关部门根据经济社会发展需要，组织制定修订职业教育专业目录、完善职业教育标准、审批备案职业学校和专业、管理并指导教材建设；人力资源和社会保障部负责统筹建立城乡劳动者职业技能培训制度，完善职业资格制度，拟订职业分类、职业技能标准等。

3. 分级管理体系健全

国家、省、市教育行政部门均设有职业教育管理机构，分级管理职业教育，保证国家职业教育政策的贯彻执行。省级政府依法可以整合优化省内设区市（县）政府的职业教育工作职责，统一管理部门，统筹省域职业教育发展。各级地方政府在中央政府规定的政策范围内，制定适合本地区实际、促进本地区职业教育发展的政策和措施，并对本地区职业教育进行指导与管理。

（三）形成多元协同的支持服务体系

1. 设立专门支撑机构

2022年，在教育部职业技术教育中心研究所的基础上，设立教育部职业教育发展中心，为教育部提供职业教育政策制订及项目实施方面的支持保障，面向社会提供公益服务，并致力于将其打造成为职业教育决策服务中心、能力建设平台、协同创新平台、交流合作平台、宣传推广平台。

2. 形成专业科研系统

机构方面，以中国教育科学研究院为首的国家及地方教育科研机构均设有专门的职业教育科研部门或岗位，一些高职学校也内设专门机构开展职业教育办学与教学研究；学科方面，以北京师范大学、华东师范大学为代表，全国50余所普通高等学校设有职业技术教育学科，从事职业教育学领域的高层次研究型人才培养，以及学科建设与研究；刊物方面，《中国职业技术教育》等4种中文核心期刊、英文期刊《Vocation，Technology & Education》、20余种专业学术期刊、164种职业学校主办期刊，成为职教研究成果发布交流的载体。

3. 各类组织协同支持

社会各界均以不同形式参与支持职业教育。中华职业教育社广泛联系国内外职业教育界和民办教育界人士宣传研究举办职业教育；中华全国总工会以工会组织为主阵地，促进产业工人技能提升、推动技术创新；中国职业技术教育学会作为全国性、学术性社会团体发挥重要智库作用；中国教育国际交流协会积极推动中国与其他国家地区职业教育的民间交流合作；教育部委托行业牵头组建的57个全国行业职业教育教学指导委员会和6个教育部职业院校教学（教育）指导委员会，对相关行业职业教育与培训开展研究咨询与指导服务。

4. 完善技能竞赛制度

连续举办16届全国职业院校技能大赛，并于2024年全面升级为世界职业院校技能大赛；自2020年起，中国每两年举办一届全国职业技能大赛。由此带动行业、地方、企业、院校各种专业竞赛蓬勃开展，构建起以校赛为基础、省赛为主体、世赛为牵引，上下衔接、内外贯通的技能竞赛体系，促进了职业教育专业建设与改革。中国已连续参加七届世界技能大赛，成绩持续提高。2024年9月结束的第47届世界技能大赛上，中国参加了全部59项比赛，获得金牌36枚、银牌9枚、铜牌4枚和8个优胜奖，位居金牌榜、奖牌榜和团体总分首位，获奖的66名选手中，59名选手来自职业学校。

5. 举办职教活动周

自2015年起，国务院将每年5月份的第二周设为职业教育活动周，在全国范围内跨部门集中宣传职业教育的法律法规、方针政策、建设成果、社会成效、改革经验和典型人物等。累计已有7.45万所职业学校、超过1亿名学生、3万家企业和1.3亿社会人员参与，极大促进了在全社会弘扬劳动光荣、技能宝贵、创造伟大的时代风尚，形成"崇尚一技之长、不唯学历凭能力"的良好氛围。

二、形成中国特色职业教育发展模式

经过多年实践，中国逐渐形成了"政府主导、学校主体、产教融合"的职业教育发展模式。2022年，中共中央办公厅、国务院办公厅《关于深化现代职业教育体系建设改革的意见》提出"一体、两翼、五重点"改革新举措，以建立部省协同推进机制为切入点，设计了央地互动、区域联动、政行企校协同的职业教育改革新机制，着力营造制度供给充分、条件保障有力、产教深度融合的职教发展新生态。

（一）探索省域现代职业教育体系建设新模式

"一体"，即探索省域现代职业教育体系建设新模式。教育部依据国家区域发展规划和重大战略，选择与有条件基础、改革意愿和成熟设计的省（自治区、直辖市）协同试点，将产教融合、职普融通等作为改革方向，优化地方职业教育发展的制度环境和生态，形成可复制、可推广的新经验新范式，以点上的改革突破带动面上的质量提升。

2023年，教育部与广西壮族自治区、天津市、山东省、新疆维吾尔自治区、黑龙江省、浙江省、重庆市和湖南省8个省、自治区和直辖市共建省域现代职业教育体系建设新模式，立足共建省（自治区、直辖市）的条件特点任务，分别出台省域现代职业教育体系建设改革实施方案（表1-1），共同改革创新发展职业教育的体制机制，促进发展与地方产业结构匹配、与区域发展协调、富有地方特色的本地现代职业教育，更好服务区域经济社会。

表1-1　8个省域现代职业教育体系建设改革实施方案

序号	省、自治区和直辖市	部省联合发文名称	印发时间
1	广西壮族自治区	《推动产教集聚融合　打造面向东盟的职业教育开放合作创新高地实施方案》	2023年4月19日

续表

序号	省、自治区和直辖市	部省联合发文名称	印发时间
2	天津市	《探索现代职业教育体系建设改革新模式实施方案》	2023年5月8日
3	山东省	《关于促进职业教育提质升级赋能绿色低碳高质量发展先行区建设的实施意见》	2023年5月19日
4	新疆维吾尔自治区	《关于深化现代职业教育体系建设改革的实施意见》	2023年7月13日
5	黑龙江省	《推进职业教育与产业集群集聚融合服务龙江振兴发展实施方案》	2023年10月18日
6	浙江省	《加快职业教育提级赋能服务共同富裕示范区建设实施方案》	2023年11月28日
7	重庆市	《深化现代职业教育体系改革服务成渝地区双城经济圈建设实施方案》	2023年12月27日
8	湖南省	《关于进一步深化职业教育产教融合服务国家重要先进制造业高地建设的实施方案》	2023年12月29日

（二）建设市域产教联合体和行业产教融合共同体

"两翼"，即市域产教联合体和行业产教融合共同体。教育部支持省级、市级人民政府以产业园区为基础，打造兼具人才培养、创新创业、促进产业经济高质量发展功能的政行企校共同建设的产教联合体，推动各类主体深度参与职业教育。在重点行业和重点领域，支持龙头企业和普通高校、职业学校牵头，组建学校、科研机构、上下游企业等共同参与的行业产教融合共同体，为行业提供稳定的人力资源和技术支撑。

2023年，教育部首批在全国遴选建设了28个市域产教联合体，2024年新设国家市域产教联合体6个，带动237个省级市域产教联合体建设，提升了职业教育与地方经济结合的"紧密度"；分别于2023年7月和2024年7月成立国家轨道交通装备行业、国家有色金属行业2个国家级行业产教融合共同体，带动各行各业建设行业产教融合共同体超过1,100个，提升了职业教育与行业发展需要的"适配度"。两个国家级行业产教融合共同体通过组织普通高校、职业学校、企业等共组教学团队、共建教学资源，将重点建设80个专业、开发270门专业核心课程和330种优质教材、建设200个生产实践中心和280个生产性实训项目。

（三）提升学校关键办学能力

针对影响职业教育改革发展的痛点难点问题，教育部从标准、专业、课程、教材、教师、基地等职业学校关键办学能力建设入手，着力提升办学质量，取得显著成效（表1-2）。

表1-2 职业学校关键办学能力提升成果一览表

类别	类项	成果
国家标准体系	学校标准	8份
	专业简介	1,349份
	专业教学标准	987份
	中职公共基础课程标准	10份
	岗位实习标准	151份
	教师标准	5份
高水平学校	中国特色高水平高职学校	197所
	优质中职学校	2,121所
高水平专业/群	高水平高职专业/群	253个
	优质中职专业	4,198个
精品课程	国家级在线精品课	1,160门
	国家级职业教育专业教学资源库	203个
优质教材	首批"十四五"职业教育国家规划教材	7,251种
	国家教材建设奖优秀教材	315种

类别	类项	成果
高水平"双师"	国家级职业教育教师创新团队	511个
	新时代职业学校名师（名匠）名校长培养	260人
	"双师型"教师培训基地和校长培训基地	213个
	全国职教教师企业实践基地	202个
产教融合实践中心	支持地方建设公共实训基地	327个

1. 建成"三位一体"的国家标准体系

教育部牵头会同有关部门，统筹规划、开发国家职业教育标准，形成了包括学校标准、教学标准、教师标准三种类型的国家职业教育标准体系，为提升职业学校关键办学能力设定基准线。分层次分类型制订《本科层次职业学校设置标准（试行）》《残疾人中等职业学校设置标准》等8个职业学校建设标准，规范引导职业学校办学；紧密对接行业标准、职业标准、岗位标准，凝聚行业组织、骨干企业、研究机构力量，制定并发布了1,349个专业简介、987个专业教学标准、10门中职公共基础课课程标准、151个岗位实习标准等国家教学标准；出台实施4个教师标准。在此基础上，山东省开发了322个专业教学标准和147个中职、高职与应用型本科相衔接的课程标准，江苏省制定了106个专业指导性人才培养方案和520门五年制高职核心课课程标准（图1-7）。

2. 建成一批高水平职业学校和专业（群）

高职方面，2019年教育部遴选建设197所国家级高水平高等职业学校、253个高水平专业群（以下简称"双高计划"），带动各地立项建设823所省域高水平高等职业学校和1,876个高水平专业群。中职方面，已建成近千所国家中等职业教育改革发展示范学校，2,000所中等职业学校达到省级骨干学校建设标准，国家级、省级示范（骨干）学校等优质资源惠及50%以上在校生。依托高水平学校和高水平专业建设，培养了大批产业急需、技艺高超的高素质技能人才，为落实国家区域发展战略、产业升级、企业技术创新提供了支撑。

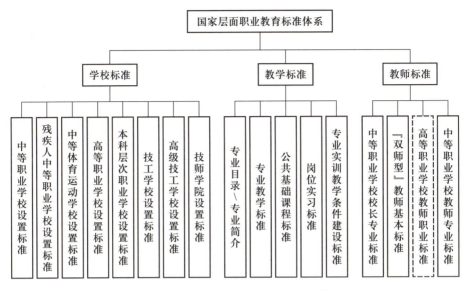

图1-7 国家职业教育标准体系图[1]

五年来，"双高计划"共投入中央财政资金106.26亿元，撬动地方、举办方、企业、学校等投入资金638.91亿元。项目学校办学条件得到明显改善，办学质量大幅提高，中央财政建设项目绩效明显。

3. 建成一批精品课程和优质教材

建成国家级在线精品课1,160门，国家级职业教育专业教学资源库203个；确定首批"十四五"职业教育国家规划教材7,251种，315种职业教育教材入选全国教材建设奖；上线"国家职业教育智慧教育平台"，聚合各类优质教学资源715万余条，包括虚拟仿真资源1,777个、在线精品课10,389门、专业教学资源库1,559个；用户覆盖1,500余所高职院校、3,000余所中职学校、3,200余家企事业单位，实际服务超过2,300万人，总浏览量突破45亿次。

4. 培养了一批高水平"双师型"教师

高水平大学、头部企业和职业学校联合，共建213个"双师型"教师培

1　高等职业学校教师职业标准正在研制中。

训基地和校长培训基地，202个全国职教教师企业实践基地发布教师实践项目1,792个、提供实践岗位两万余个；职业学校教师素质提高计划完成国家级培训13.6万人次、省级培训9.2万人次，实施80个职教国培示范项目；分三批建设511个国家级职业教育教师创新团队，覆盖全国各省级教育行政单位。启动实施"新时代职业学校名师（名匠）名校长培养计划"，确定首批培养对象260余人；2023年全国中等职业教育"双师型"专任教师占专业（技能）课程专任教师的比例达到56.71%[1]。

5. 建成一批开放型区域产教融合实践中心

截至2023年底，地方自主建设了327个公共实训基地，累计培训近300万人次。比如，山东省以政府主导、多元投入，16个市每市建设一个开放型大型区域产教融合实践中心，差异化建设分中心194个，构成了技术领先、有效共享的实践基地体系；江西省建设区域产教融合实践中心52个、职业教育虚拟仿真示范实训基地27个。

三、高质量人才培养的能力持续提升

为满足现代化产业体系建设对技能人才培养质量的更高要求，中国坚持落实立德树人根本任务、创新技能人才培养模式，人才培养能力和质量持续提高。

（一）德技并修机制更加健全

1. 德育工作更加深入

将理想信念、思想道德、工匠精神等有机融入专业知识学习和技能训练全

1　数据来源：2023年全国教育事业发展统计公报。

过程，推出200门职业教育课程思政示范课、11个教学研究示范中心，全国职业学校教师参与课程思政集体备课近40万人次，学生的思想政治素质和职业道德素质得到加强，社会公德、家庭美德、职业道德、个人品德有效提升。

2. 活动育人不断丰富

连续21年举办"文明风采"活动，提高学生思想道德素质和综合素养。2022年以来，持续开展技能传承中华优秀传统文化活动、"未来工匠"读书行动、"劳模工匠进校园"行动等"技能成才　强国有我"系列活动，年均参与学生超5,000万人次，"技能成才、技能报国"形成广泛共识。

3. "三全育人"持续推进

坚持"全员、全过程、全方位"育人，保证思想政治和德育工作全覆盖、不断线；持续培育和践行社会主义核心价值观，塑造学生健全的人格和高尚的人品。建设3,100余个班主任工作室，5万余名教师参与，发挥中职学校班主任在管理育人中的主力作用。

（二）对接产业的专业教学体系更加完善

1. 依据产业需求修订专业目录

2021年，教育部全面修订职业教育专业目录，一体化设计中等职业教育、高等职业教育专科、高等职业教育本科不同层次的专业结构和对应关系，修订后的目录共设置19个专业大类、97个专业类、1,349个专业，其中，中职专业358个、高职专科专业744个、高职本科专业247个（图1-8）。国家战略性新兴产业、现代服务业重点领域、数字产业化和产业数字化、乡村振兴等领域成为专业设置的重点。目录覆盖国民经济各领域，与第一产业对应的专业占比4.20%、与第二产业对应的专业占比38.70%、与第三产业对应的专业占比57.10%，目录专业结构与2021年三次产业在国民生产总值中的占比（第一产业7.30%、第二产业39.40%、第三产业53.30%）及发展趋势基本匹配（图1-9）。

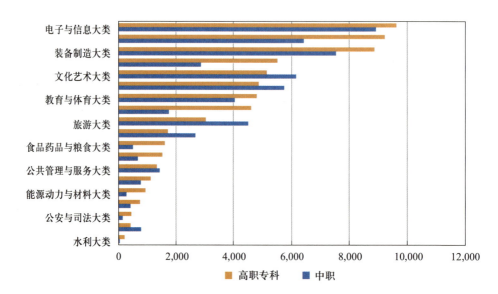

图1-8　2024年中职、高职专科专业布点数（单位：个）[1]

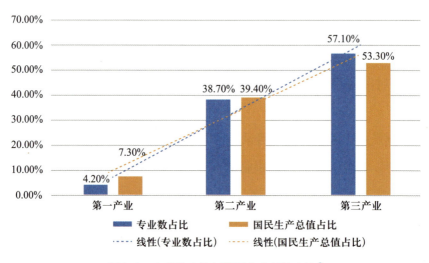

图1-9　专业数占比与国民生产总值占比[2]

1　按照《国民经济行业分类》（GB/T 4754—2017）对《职业教育专业目录（2021年）》进行分类统计。

2　按照《国民经济行业分类》（GB/T 4754—2017）对《职业教育专业目录（2021年）》进行分类统计。

2. 建立专业动态调整机制

各行业职业教育教学指导委员会定期发布《行业人才需求与职业院校专业设置指导报告》。教育部与省级教育行政部门联动实施专业预警和动态调整机制，在此基础上逐步扩大学校自主设置特色专业的权限。2012年以来，高等职业教育专业点年均调整幅度超过12%。2024年高等职业教育新增专业点6,068个、撤并专业点5,052个，调整幅度达17%。

3. 规范专业人才培养方案制订

要求职业学校以国家教学标准为基础，综合区域发展需求、办学特色和专业实际，自主制订专业人才培养方案，合理确定专业培养目标，明确学生的知识能力素质要求，持续提升学生的职业适应能力和可持续发展能力。学校通过规范公共基础课和专业（技能）课设置，加强学生职业能力和职业精神的培养；实践性教学学时占总学时的比例超过50%。通过校企合作、数智融合等方式开发课程超过14万门。支持学生在取得学历证书的同时，取得有关领域职业资格证书、职业技能等级证书、培训证书。

（三）技能人才培养模式持续创新

1. 持续推行学徒制人才培养

以现代学徒制、企业新型学徒制为抓手，持续深化产教融合，推进校企"双元"育人。2014年以来，教育部分三批在全国布局558个国家级现代学徒制试点项目，覆盖专业点1,000多个，惠及学生超过10万人；人力资源和社会保障部推动技工学校联合企业广泛开展企业新型学徒制，推动开展岗位技能提升、转岗转业培训，提高企业员工技能。

2. 探索课堂教学形态改革

创新"园区课堂""农场课堂""车间课堂"等组织形式，在生产环境中培养学生的职业能力、职业精神和职业素养。广泛采用情境教学、案例教学、项目教学等符合技能人才培养的模式，灵活采用集体教学、小组教学、个别辅导等差异化教学方式，让不同禀赋学生找到适合自身的学习形式，寻求适合自身发展的途径和空间。

3. 数字赋能技能人才培养

73.24%的职业学校接入省市级教育专网，57.77%的职业学校实现校园网络完全覆盖。2015年以来，教育部分五批建设"职业院校数字校园"实验（试点）校1,152所。接近55%的职业学校教师开展混合式教学，通过创设"虚实融合""情境模拟""人机协同"等支撑智慧学习的教学场景，打造教学内容、课程资源、工作场景相融合的"全景课堂"。

（四）质量评价体系持续完善

构建国家、地方、学校三级评价体系，引导职业学校坚持正确办学方向、保障教育教学质量、增强职业教育吸引力。国家层面，持续迭代评价指标，2004年以来，先后开展五次全国性职业学校专项评估、督导、检查，职业教育内部质量保证制度和运行机制逐渐完善；建立国家、省、学校三级职业教育质量年度报告制度，展示职业教育成就风采，主动接受社会监督。地方层面，创新开展彰显地方特色的评估评价实践，比如，上海市建立周期性学校自主诊改与市级抽样复核相结合的制度，湖南省建立高职院校专业技能教学水平抽查测试制度，辽宁省建立星级专业评估制度等。学校层面，逐渐形成比较健全的职业学校校内质量保障体系、教学工作诊断与改进机制。

（五）学生及社会满意度持续攀升

1. 毕业生满意度超过92%

调查显示，2023年度全国职业学校毕业生满意度超过92%，其中，中职毕业生满意度94.42%、高职专科毕业生满意度93.10%、高职本科毕业生满意度92.70%。73.78%的高职学生愿意推荐亲朋好友就读的高等职业学校，"双高计划"建设高等职业学校推荐度达到81.68%（图1-10）。

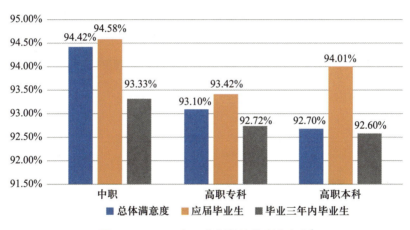

图1-10　2023年职业学校毕业生满意度[1]

2. 学生家长对职业教育满意度超过95%

2023年，全国6,000余所中高等职业学校学生家长满意度调查显示，家长整体满意度95.23%，中职、高职专科和高职本科学生家长满意度分别为95.42%、94.54%、95.19%（图1-11）。

3. 用人单位对毕业生满意度超过93%

2023年，全国6,000余所中高等职业学校毕业生所在单位满意度调查显示，用人单位对中职、高职专科和高职本科毕业生满意度分别为94.37%、

1　数据来源：中国职业教育质量年度报告数据采集平台。

95.94%和97.30%，较2022年均有提升。用人单位对职业学校毕业生职业素养、职业能力、工作岗位适应能力认可度较高（图1-12）。

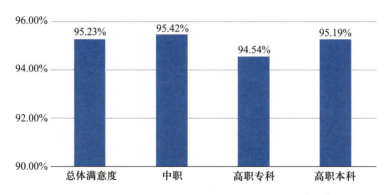

图1-11　2023年职业学校学生家长满意度[1]

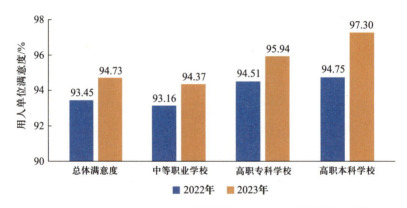

图1-12　2022—2023年职业学校毕业生所在用人单位满意度[2]

四、有力支撑经济社会高质量发展

近年来，中国职业教育积极致力提升自身在助力区域和产业发展、为产业提供技能人才支撑、促进社会公平和实现共同富裕等方面的能力和水平。

1　数据来源：中国职业教育质量年度报告数据采集平台。
2　数据来源：中国职业教育质量年度报告数据采集平台。

（一）形成服务区域发展的结构布局

1. 院校布局紧密对接省域发展需求

中国坚定职业教育重点服务区域发展的基本定位，根据需要主动建设、整合、调整中等和高等职业学校，优化省域职业学校布局。目前，全国省级行政单位均举办有职业学校，中等职业学校省均308所、高等职业学校省均52所；全国333个地级行政区划单位中有312个设有高等职业学校，每个地级行政区划单位平均5所，不少高职学校成为所在市域的唯一高校，成为推动区域经济社会健康可持续发展的持久动力（图1-13）。

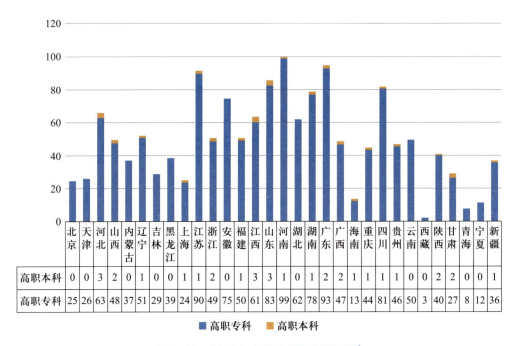

	北京	天津	河北	山西	内蒙古	辽宁	吉林	黑龙江	上海	江苏	浙江	安徽	福建	江西	山东	河南	湖北	湖南	广东	广西	海南	重庆	四川	贵州	云南	西藏	陕西	甘肃	青海	宁夏	新疆
高职本科	0	0	3	2	0	1	0	0	1	1	2	0	1	3	3	1	0	1	2	2	1	1	1	1	0	0	2	2	0	0	1
高职专科	25	26	63	48	37	51	29	39	24	90	49	75	50	61	83	99	62	78	93	47	13	44	81	46	50	3	40	27	8	12	36

■ 高职专科　■ 高职本科

图1-13　2022年各省高等职业学校数[1]

2. 集群服务国家区域一体化协调发展战略

2018年，中国启动实施区域协调发展战略，推动京津冀、长三角、粤港

1　数据来源：2022年全国教育事业发展统计公报。

澳大湾区、成渝地区双城经济圈等重点区域建设发展。其中，职业教育资源的协调与匹配是重要内容。2018年以来，全国已先后成立大湾区职业教育产教联盟、大湾区职业教育教师发展联盟、粤港澳大湾区特色职业教育园区、京津冀职业教育改革示范园区等，成为央地互动、区域联动协同平台，职业教育集群推动区域协同发展战略迈向更高水平。

（二）供给产业急需的技能人才和服务

1. 助力中国产业结构性转型升级

中国职业教育紧紧围绕新质生产力发展需要，优化专业设置、创新培养模式，以高素质劳动者供给夯实新质生产力发展基础。2023年，高等职业学校面向新一代信息技术产业、高端装备制造产业、新材料产业、生物产业等战略性新兴产业领域新增专业布点1,266个，比上年增加8.24%，毕业生105万余人（图1-14）。

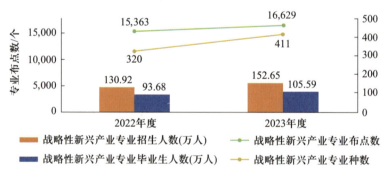

图1-14　2022—2023年度全国高等职业学校面向战略性新兴产业的专业布局[1]

2. 协同中国企业解决一线生产问题

中国职业教育立足区域产业实际，面向企业尤其是中小微企业生产经营需要，与企业协同开展技术服务、工艺改进、产品升级，推进技术开发成果产业

1　数据来源：中国职业教育质量年度报告数据采集平台。

化应用，助力解决企业一线生产问题。2023年，职业学校重点瞄准新能源汽车、智能制造、新材料等领域的技术和工艺问题，承接国家级科研项目2,700余项，比2022年增长7.52%；通过校企共建技术服务平台等方式为企业开展技术服务，累计金额超过91亿元；转让专利成果超过7,000个，涉及金额超5.40亿元（图1-15）。

图1-15　2022—2023年度高等职业学校国家级科研项目及专利转化情况[1]

（三）在脱贫攻坚和乡村振兴中发挥重要作用

1. 对接乡村振兴需求开展涉农培训

支持村干部、新型农业经营主体带头人等就地就近接受职业教育，培养了一批在乡大学生、乡村治理人才。连续举办面向农村青壮年劳动力的"普通话＋职业技能"培训。2013年起，教育部等六部门分五批认定国家级农村职业教育和成人教育示范县261个。2019年，农业农村部与教育部联合启动"百万高素质农民学历提升行动计划"，认定100多所乡村振兴人才培养优质校和农业科研院所，累计培养100万名具有较高学历的乡村振兴带头人。

1　数据来源：中国职业教育质量年度报告数据采集平台。

2. 开展农业技术推广和专业人才培养

面向一线农业生产人员开展现代农业生产等技术培训，推广应用新品种、新技术、新方法、新装备。全国274所农业类职业学校共设置农业类专业35个，高等职业学校专业布点近700个、年招生超过4万人，申报相关知识产权数量超过600项。2024年，农业农村部公布第一批全国县级优质农民田间学校534所。

3. 开展职业教育东西协作对口支援

针对地区发展不平衡等问题，2001年教育部启动教育对口支援计划，实施"东西职业学校协作全覆盖""东西中职招生协作兜底""职业学校全面参与东西劳务协作"三大行动，累计投入帮扶资金（设备）超过18亿元，共建专业点683个、实训基地338个、分校（教学点）63个，开展就业技能培训14万余人次、岗位技能提升培训16万余人次，极大地补充了西部地区高质量发展所需的技能人才。

（四）推动实现更高水平更充分就业

1. 毕业生去向落实率维持高位

中国政府把促进青年就业工作摆在突出位置，通过特色就业服务和多种去向选择，为毕业生提供丰富的就业资源和专业化就业服务。2022—2024年，中等职业学校毕业生毕业去向落实率分别为94.70%、94.44%、93.96%，高等职业学校毕业生毕业去向落实率分别为90.60%、91.88%、93.55%，总体保持在高位（图1-16）。

2. 毕业生就业质量持续提升

中国政府强化就业优先政策，关心关怀学生高质量就业，持续开展"高校书记校长访企拓岗""万企进校园""24365校园网络招聘"等专项行动，帮助毕业生实现高质量就业。近三年，高等职业学校毕业生所学专业与就业岗位对口率逐年提升，2023届毕业生达到72.17%，较2021届增长4.75%（图1-17）；2023届毕业生初次就业平均起薪4,082.20元，较2021届增长11.13%（图1-18）。

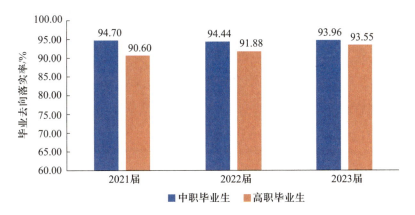

图1-16　2021—2023届中等职业学校、高等职业学校毕业生毕业去向落实率[1]

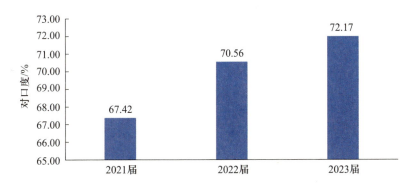

图1-17　2021—2023届高等职业学校毕业生就业对口率[2]

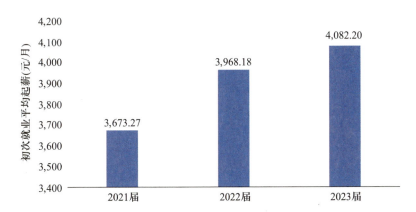

图1-18　2021—2023届高等职业学校毕业生初次就业平均起薪[3]

1　　数据来源：中国职业教育质量年度报告数据采集平台。

2　　数据来源：中国职业教育质量年度报告数据采集平台。

3　　数据来源：中国职业教育质量年度报告数据采集平台。

3. 协助退役军人高质量就业

近年来，教育部与退役军人事务部联合开展退役军人学历教育提升工作，助力107.3万名退役军人进入高职专科学校学习，支持9.5万名退役军人通过职业适应性考查评价或职业技能综合考查评价进入大学本科学习。校企合作、跨省异地培训退役军人累计超过100万人。

4. 扩大"一老一小"领域急需人才培养能力

中国职业教育积极应对社会人口结构性变化趋势，扩大"一老一小"相关专业布点和人才培养规模，开展托育服务、养老服务等职业技能培训。2021年以来，高等职业学校智慧健康养老管理、现代家政服务与管理、婴幼儿托育服务与管理等民生紧缺专业点开设数量年增长率超过5%。2024年全国高职专科备案"一老一小"相关专业点3,480余个，毕业生41.5万人。

五、成为教育国际交流合作的生力军

中国政府以创新、协调、绿色、开放、共享的新发展理念，统筹职业教育"引进来"和"走出去"，搭建国际交流合作平台，凝聚职业教育发展共识，分享中国职教方案，携手各国共同推进职业教育发展。中国职业教育"走出去"主要在亚洲和非洲等共建"一带一路"国家，以能源化工、物流管理、装备制造等专业为主，呈现出中国院校、"走出去"中资企业与国外政府、企业、院校多主体合作办学态势。

（一）积极参与全球职业教育合作

1. 与联合国教科文组织合作开展职业教育数字化、绿色化发展研究

充分发挥教育部职业教育发展中心等六家联合国教科文组织国际职业技术

教育与培训中心联络中心（UNEVOC Center），和设在深圳职业技术大学的联合国教科文组织职业技术教育数字化教席等的作用，围绕职业教育数字化、绿色技能培养、国际交流合作等议题，与联合国教科文组织有关机构和成员开展合作研究。

2. 与联合国儿童基金会合作提升职业学校学生"核心能力"

由教育部职业教育发展中心牵头，面向职业学校学生开展青少年"核心能力提升"项目，通过提升学生的自我认知、问题解决、人际关系、情绪管理、批判性思维和创造性思维、绿色技能和数字技能等核心能力，帮助学生更好地适应未来的社会和经济环境。目前项目已进入第三个周期（每个周期五年），覆盖19个省份的134所职业学校。组织职业学校学生代表参加联合国驻华系统"绿色未来她力量"亚太峰会活动及"绿色技能"青年咨商对话等。

3. 与世界技能组织合作助推世界技能事业高质量发展

连续选派选手参加世界技能大赛，累计取得57金32银24铜的优异成绩，并在2017、2019、2022、2024年赛事中荣登金牌榜第一，向全世界展现中国青年精益求精、积极进取的精神风貌。与世界技能组织合作，筹备第48届世界技能大赛。

（二）搭建国际交流合作平台

主动聚合国内外优质职业教育资源，组建国际联盟、举办国际论坛、开展多元合作，已形成的区域性合作机制包括："一带一路"职教联盟、未来非洲——中非职业教育合作计划、金砖国家职业教育联盟、中国——中东欧国家职业学校产教联盟、中国——东盟职业教育联合会、丝绸之路亚欧院校（职教）联盟、陆海新通道职业教育国际合作联盟、澜沧江——湄公河职业教育联盟等。举办世界职业技术教育发展大会，创建集"会—盟—奖—赛—展"于一体的职业教育国际公共服务品牌。

 专栏

习近平主席向2022年世界职业技术教育发展大会致贺信

职业教育与经济社会发展紧密相连，对促进就业创业、助力经济社会发展、增进人民福祉具有重要意义。中国积极推动职业教育高质量发展，支持中外职业教育交流合作。中方愿同世界各国一道，加强互学互鉴、共建共享，携手落实全球发展倡议，为加快落实联合国2030年可持续发展议程贡献力量。

（三）主动分享中国方案

中国在大力发展职业教育过程中，既积极学习借鉴国际先进经验，也主动将自身经验分享给世界。

1. 共创职教国际品牌项目

目前，有27个省（自治区、直辖市）的近300所职业学校与70多个国家（地区）合作设立了约400个办学机构和项目，涌现出"鲁班工坊""中文工坊""班·墨学院""现代工匠学院""丝路学院"等一批境外办学品牌（表1-3）。

表1-3　地方代表性职业教育国际品牌一览表

序号	品牌名称	发起省份	首创时间	合作国家数量	设立数量
1	丝路学院	浙江	2016年	34个	52个
2	郑和学院	江苏	2018年	9个	9个
3	海丝学院	福建	2019年	17个	20个
4	班·墨学院	山东	2023年	17个	34个
5	墨子工坊	辽宁	2023年	14个	16个
6	中国–东盟现代工匠学院	广西	2023年	10个	17个

2. 共建职业学校

在项目合作基础上，中国职业教育开始探索与共建"一带一路"国家和地区合作建设职业学校，为当地培养高素质技能人才。比如，南京工业职业技术大学与柬埔寨柬华理事总会合作共建柬华应用科技大学，开设招生专业7个，为当地培养校企合作订单班学生3,000余人；天津职业技术师范大学与埃塞俄比亚共建埃塞俄比亚联邦职业技术教育与培训学院，开设22个本科专业，共培养5,000余名毕业生。

 案例

柬华应用科技大学

2023年12月20日，由南京工业职业技术大学与柬埔寨柬华理事总会合作共建的柬华应用科技大学正式成立。柬华应用科技大学以培养柬埔寨本土技能人才为办学宗旨，采用"4+0""2+2""3+1"等模式开展高职本科学历教育。学生通过四年的学习，可同时获得中国和柬埔寨两国的学历和学位证书，目前开设了新能源发电工程技术、汽车服务工程技术、网络工程技术、电子商务、现代物流管理、旅游管理、机械电子工程技术七个本科专业。柬华应用科技大学的运行，不仅提升了中国共享职业教育方案的规格，也在区域职业教育共同体上做出了新的尝试和探索。

3. 为合作国家培养大量技能人才

在亚欧非三大洲合作建成30余个鲁班工坊，学历教育累计培养学生近万人，实施职业培训超过3.1万人次。中国有色金属行业牵手10所中国职业学校成立的中赞职业技术学院，2023年首届毕业生近90%被当地中资企业录用；广西农业职业技术大学通过建设中老合作试验站，培训当地农业技术员近2,000人次、农民1万多人次，推广的67个优良品种种植面积4万多亩，获得老挝农林部突出贡献奖，成为中老合作的典范。

4. 国际影响力不断扩大

中国职业学校凭借真诚的合作和优质的资源逐渐得到所在国的认可。乌兹别克斯坦、老挝、越南、斯里兰卡等多国领导人在与中国领导人会面时均对中国职业教育实力表示肯定，希望学习借鉴中国职业教育发展经验。2022年世界职业技术教育发展大会上，埃塞俄比亚劳动与技能部部长穆费里亚特·卡米勒·艾哈迈德发表主旨演讲时表示，希望中国扩大在该国设立的鲁班工坊规模，使其"能覆盖到埃塞俄比亚各个地区"。肯尼亚总统鲁托访华出席第三届"一带一路"国际合作高峰论坛时表示：感谢中国自2014年起在人力资源培训等方面给予肯方的重要支持，肯尼亚140所院校从中获益，受训人数由9万人增至35万人，为经济社会发展提供了重要的技能支撑。

第二编　基本经验

中国职业教育与中国经济发展同向同行，与各国职业教育互学互鉴。改革开放四十余年，特别是2012年以来的探索前行，锻造出中国职业教育的优势，形成了发展职业教育的中国经验。

一、充分发挥政府的统筹和推动作用

中国将职业教育视作重要的公共服务产品，把职业教育摆在优先发展的战略地位，不断加大制度创新、政策供给、投入力度，更好地支持和推动职业教育发展。

1. 依法治教，健全法规体系

《中华人民共和国职业教育法》（2022年修订，以下称《职教法》）明确了职业教育作为一种教育类型的法律地位，明确了各级政府、各级各类职业学校的法定职责，以及行业企业实施职业教育的法定义务。《职教法》颁布以来，省级职业教育条例及有关专项法规纷纷出台。山东省《职业教育条例》要求推动企业、学校、科研机构等主体共同开展人才培养、科研攻关和技术研发服务；天津市《职业教育产教融合促进条例》支持组建区域产教联合体、产业链产教融合共同体，并推进实体化运行。以《职教法》为引领，国家和地方相关法律法规、部门规章、规范性文件等共同构成的职业教育法律法规体系持续完善，保证了职业教育沿着法治化轨道平稳发展。

2. 高位统筹，加大制度供给

通过定期召开全国性的职业教育工作会议、建立各层级跨部门联席会议制度、建立面向公众的重大决策征求意见制度等，统一思想、凝聚共识、形成合力，引领职业教育改革方向，为职业教育注入动力。2012年以来，国家层面召开两次职业教育工作会议，国务院制定出台4份职业教育专项改革文件，教育部出台27份职业教育改革文件，相关改革举措覆盖职业教育顶层设计、多元治理、人才培养、政策激励、制度保障等多个领域，在职业教育发展的重要节点明确改革方向与发展战略，形成了中国职业教育改革发展的"四梁八柱"。

3. 央地协同，创新部省共建的改革发展机制

支持地方因地制宜先行先试，分别选择东中西部有基础、有意愿的省级和地市级政府共同推进关键改革。2019年以来，国务院连续4年对职业教育改革成效明显省份给予激励（每年5个左右）。继2020年教育部先后与山东、甘肃、江西等11个省份共建职业教育创新发展高地，构建点线面结合、南北呼应、东中西联动的改革格局，把深化职业教育改革落实到整省和城市群之后，2023年起在8个省份整省开展推进现代职业教育体系建设改革试点，进一步创新央地互动、区域联动、多方协同的发展机制。这些机制极大地激发了地方发展和创新职业教育的积极性，推动职业教育围绕服务区域发展战略，实现差异化、特色化发展。

4. 加大投入，支持社会力量广泛平等参与职业教育

坚持职业教育的公益属性，公办职业教育规模始终保持主体地位，极大地保障了每个人公平享有职业教育的权利。2012年以来，职业教育公共财政投入稳步增长。高等职业教育投入由2012年的1,410亿元，增长至2017年的

2,023亿元，至2023年达到3,630亿元；中等职业教育投入2017年为2,319亿元，2023年增长至3,309亿元。同时，中国政府注重统筹办学资源，采取政府补贴、基金奖励、捐资激励等扶持措施，多措并举鼓励和支持社会资本举办职业教育。截至2023年，社会力量举办的中等职业学校达到2,128所，占比25%；高等职业学校达到396所，占比30%。

二、注重职业教育与经济社会协同发展

将发展职业教育纳入国民经济和社会发展总体规划，立足区域内的产业布局和企业发展需求，动态调整专业设置和人才培养规格，行业、企业等用人主体与职业学校联合开展人才培养、技术研发和社会服务。

1. 建立国家层面的产业人才供需发布和匹配机制

全国行业职业教育教学指导委员会定期组织研究并发布人才需求与专业设置指导报告，人力资源和社会保障部门发布不同行业技能人才供需情况。教育部按照现代化产业体系对技能人才结构的实际需求，依据国民经济行业分类、职业分类大典、新职业目录，在科学分析产业、职业、岗位、专业关系的基础上，编制和定期修订职业教育专业目录。

2. 地方政府和职业学校及时响应区域经济发展变化

地方教育行政部门对标区域产业发展规划，以专业备案、绩效评价、资金划拨等方式，引导职业学校办学资源、专业设置与区域产业结构相匹配。各级各类职业学校通过成立专业建设指导委员会，引入企业参与人才培养，定期访企拓岗，了解企业需求，缩短对企业用人需求的响应时间。比如，安徽省"十四五"时期规划重点发展新能源汽车、人工智能、先进光伏和新型储能等新兴产业，为此，安徽省教育厅主动出台专业对接和预警机制等十项措施，对服

务新兴产业和未来产业的专业进行奖补。目前，安徽省服务十大新兴产业的职业教育专业占比达58.12%，技能人才服务支撑产业创新发展的能力得到提升。

3. 鼓励职业学校服务企业技术改进与升级

支持职业学校通过引进高水平师资和企业技术人员、提升服务产业发展创新的成果在教师绩效评价中的权重等，在助力区域企业转型升级、技术改进、产品升级、工艺优化、推广应用等方面发挥支持作用。比如，杭州职业技术学院通过与杭州西奥电梯有限公司合作，联合攻关解决超长跨度扶梯、电梯智慧监管平台构建等技术难题，不仅提升了企业的市场竞争力，也使学校的人才培养和技术服务得到了业界认可，相关专业的学生就业率达到98.59%。

三、着力创新产教融合、工学结合的人才培养模式

中国职业教育始终坚持产教融合、校企合作，坚持工学结合、知行合一，注重构建校企协同育人生态，建立健全职业学校与企业的制度化联系机制，以真实生产情境培养学生的实战本领和适应能力。

1. 以行业产教融合共同体和市域产教联合体为载体推进产教融合

行业产教融合共同体注重发挥央企国企、地方龙头企业、链主企业的跨区域引领作用，集中行业优质资源整体提升产业人才培养质量。以中国中车集团有限公司、中国铝业集团有限公司等为代表的大型国企央企积极行动，以校企技术、人才、资源、文化融合为路径，搭平台、建机制、强措施，构建了"校企融为一体、产教充分融合、育训有机结合、校企协同育人"的产教融合新格局，为龙头企业参与举办高质量职业教育提供了范本。市域产教联合体要求发挥产业园区政府的统筹作用，推动园区企业和相关学校、院所合作，开展技术攻关、人才培养，提升职业学校服务地方经济发展的能力和精准度。以晋江经

济开发区为依托园区建立的晋江市域产教联合体，是全国目前唯一在县域建设的国家级市域产教联合体，在校生规模已达5.8万人，2023年培养全日制毕业生1.9万名、开展社会培训5.6万人次，促成产学研合作项目1,289个，投资额超10亿元，为晋江各类企业提供多层次、全周期的技能人才支撑和技术服务。

2. 以产教融合型城市和产教融合型企业建设为抓手促进校企合作

中国构建"金融＋财政＋土地＋信用"组合式激励，吸引重大产业所在城市和行业龙头企业支持和参与职业教育办学，国家发改委已经认定21个国家产教融合试点城市，教育部认定299个示范性职业教育集团（联盟），各地培育产教融合型企业4,600多家。一大批行业组织和行业协会积极参与产教融合工作，初步形成了城市为节点、行业为支点、企业为重点的校企合作推进机制。

3. 以校企全过程对接机制实现工学结合、知行合一

职业学校普遍采用校企联合招生、联合培养、联合评价、岗位成才的方式，实现学校培养与企业用工无缝对接。学习者既是学校的学生，也是企业的员工，既可以享受学校教学资源和学生资助等在校生政策，又可以在企业工作并享受企业提供的工作津贴。校企双方根据企业岗位真实工作任务，共同制订人才培养方案，共同开发课程和教材。学校教师和企业师傅组成导师团队共同承担教学任务，按需有序安排学生在学校和企业、课堂和岗位的学习实践，提高了学校培养的针对性、适用性，解决了企业用人适配度低、上岗后培训成本高等问题。

四、把质量建设作为促进发展的核心内容

中国职业教育始终坚持立德树人、德技并修，以教学改革、"双师型"队

伍建设、数字化转型等内涵建设为抓手，提高职业学校人才培养质量。

1. 把立德树人成效作为检验职业学校办学质量的根本标准

中国始终坚持把促进人的全面发展作为职业教育的首要目标，加强标准引领和政府督导，通过国家统一的公共基础课课程标准建设，为学生提供高质量的通识教育课程，保证学校教育的育人功能。各级各类职业学校坚持育人为本、德育为先，将学生践行社会主义核心价值观情况作为综合素质评价重要内容。学校、行业和企业通力合作，通过完善职业学校师资队伍培养培训机制、健全职业学校学生心理服务体系、建立奖助学体系等，为促进学生德智体美劳全面发展提供支撑条件。

2. 注重以标准和项目推动质量提升

建立健全职业教育标准体系，发挥标准在规范人才培养、深化产教融合、保障发展质量中的基础性、引领性作用，鼓励支持职业学校基于标准办出特色。发挥国家项目促进跨部门协作、撬动地方投入、激发动力、强化导向的功能。近年来，国家层面实施的高水平高职院校和专业群建设计划、国家精品在线开放课程、职业教育专业教学资源库建设、职业学校教师素质提高计划、国家级职业教育教师教学创新团队、教师教学能力比赛等综合和专项改革项目，有效提升了职业学校的关键办学能力和自主发展能力。

3. 数字化赋能职业教育质量提升

职业教育数字化的核心目标是提升职业教育质量和效率，培养适应数字化时代需求的高素质技能人才。在数字化进程中，中国坚持系统观念，注重系统集成，既有长远的战略规划，又注重分阶段、有步骤地推进实施。2022年提出联结为先、内容为本、合作为要（简称"3C"，即Connection、Content、Cooperation），开始逐步迈向集成化、智能化、国际化（简称"3I"，即Integrated、Intelligent、International），稳步推动职业教育数字化向纵深发展。

同时，积极运用云计算、大数据、人工智能等先进技术，推动教学内容、方法和手段的数字化升级，提升学生的学习体验和效果。2022年上线的"国家智慧教育平台"荣获联合国教科文组织教育信息化奖，是中国教育数字化战略的核心成果与集大成者。

4. 注重通过竞赛和评价建立常态化的质量提升机制

通过组织高质量的全国性赛事，促进国家标准在人才培养中落地，激发职业学校改革创新动力。近年来，以全国职业院校技能大赛、国家级教学成果奖、全国教材建设奖等为代表的职教领域重大赛事和奖项，推出了一批具有原创性和开拓性的教学改革成果。中国职业学校自身的常态化周期性教学工作诊断与改进机制建设，则推动职业学校根据自身办学理念、办学定位、人才培养目标，自主开展多层面多维度的诊断与改进，不断健全校内教学质量保障体系。

五、在互学互鉴和共享共赢中深化国际交流合作

1. 构建互学互鉴职业教育平台

改革开放四十余年，中国政府、学校和民间机构先后与德国、英国、澳大利亚等国家建立合作关系，积极学习职业教育办学先进国家经验，博采众长，特别是学习技能人才培养规律、课程建设模式、教学方法改革、校企合作机制和制度建设等方面的最新研究与实践成果，与中国实践相结合，逐步形成自身的理论研究成果和办学经验。在此基础上，搭建集"会—盟—奖—赛—展"为一体的全球职业教育平台，邀约各国同仁分享发展经验、探讨发展路径。

2. 共享职业教育发展成果

通过"世界职教发展联盟""世界职业技术教育发展大会"等平台和合作

机制，积极参与全球职业教育治理。将职业教育合作与国际产能合作、减贫合作、减排合作相结合，采取学历教育和职业培训相结合的方式，分享中国职业教育教学模式、教育技术和教育标准，通过建设培训中心、提供先进教学设备，组织中国教师和技术人员为合作国培养技能人才，形成了"鲁班工坊""中文工坊"等一批共创的职业教育合作品牌，使中国成为职业教育全球公共产品的重要供给者。

第三编　战略任务

当前，中国已经步入进一步全面深化改革、推进中国式现代化的新阶段，确立了2035年建成教育强国的奋斗目标。中国将着力构建职普融通、产教融合的职业教育体系，进一步推动职业教育与产业结合、与地方和政府政策结合、与社会区域结构结合、与个人终身学习结合，致力培养更多高技能人才、能工巧匠、大国工匠。

一、提升职业教育服务国家发展战略的能力

发展新质生产力必须紧紧依靠高素质劳动者，需要职业教育扎根区域、融入产业，加快培养传统产业升级、新兴产业壮大、未来产业成长所需的高技能人才。

1. 进一步增强职业教育与区域经济的"紧密度"

服务区域经济社会发展是职业教育的重要任务，应在办学定位、服务方向、专业结构、社会贡献方面主动对标地方需要，强化与地方经济社会发展的联动，以服务求发展、以贡献求支持，不求最大，但求最优，但求适应社会需要。根据所在区域的产业结构、资源禀赋和发展阶段，主动融入京津冀、长三角、粤港澳大湾区、成渝双城经济圈等国家主体功能区发展，更好地服务省

域、市域经济社会发展。

2. 进一步增强职业教育与产业需要的"适配度"

中国产业体系门类齐全、规模庞大，拥有较为完整、具有韧性的产业链。职业教育应紧扣产业链各个环节，聚焦先进制造业、数字产业等重点产业集群、重点行业和重点领域，强化制造、装调、操作和运维等岗位相关技能人才培养；推动产业资源与教育资源的互通流动、校企协同育人与技术创新的良性互动，及时根据产业发展需要调整专业和人才培养结构，实现技能型人力资源的有效供给。

3. 进一步提升职业学校办学能力和服务水平

应坚持"办学能力高水平、产教融合高质量"的职业学校发展导向，从注重办学条件改善和自我循环发展的小逻辑，转向更加注重服务产业发展、服务社会发展的大逻辑，进一步聚焦服务国家战略、融入区域发展、促进产业升级；进一步深化改革、提升办学实力，根据技术迭代、产业升级、社会变化等因素，动态优化专业、课程、教材、师资、实训基地，从知识传授、传统技能训练向提升综合技能、数字技能转变。

二、职普融通拓展学生成长成才通道

中国的人口结构变化、高等教育普及化，使人们接受教育的渠道和选择更趋多元，需要职业教育秉持面向人人、公平全纳、有教无类、因材施教的理念，普惠化、均衡化、优质化、终身化，服务学习者全面可持续发展。

1. 注重职业启蒙教育

应进一步推进职业教育与普通教育渗透融合，让普通中小学学生在劳动和职业体验中培养劳动观念、职业意识，从小培养学生学习掌握技能的兴趣爱好，感悟技能的价值、职业的方向，为学生未来职业发展与人生规划播下理想的"种子"，为构建成功的职业生涯奠定基础。

2. 满足学生多样化发展需求

初中后教育多样化是教育体系的成熟度、灵活性、包容性的具体体现。应建立多样的职业教育与普通教育连接的通道和培养形式，为学生多次选择和多样化的人才培养提供机会和载体；健全高中阶段和本科阶段的融通模式，服务学生适应未来社会的多元化挑战。

3. 以评价改革助推学生发展

持续畅通技能人才成长渠道，完善和全面推广"文化素质+职业技能"职教高考[1]制度，保证技能人才培养方向；增加行业企业评价权重，探索建立适合全面评价学生综合素质和职业能力的评价体系，以评价改革为牵引，提升技能人才培养质量的社会认可度。

三、助力实现共同富裕

职业教育能够改善社会人力资本存量，服务人民幸福生活，需要在促进就业、扩大中等收入群体、服务乡村全面振兴、促进城乡共同繁荣、丰富人民精神文化生活等方面持续发挥作用。

1. 增强职业教育促进社会就业的基础性作用

就业是最大的民生，职业教育与培训是促进就业的最直接手段，应统筹职

1　职教高考是相对于普通高考而言的一种高等学校招生考试制度，采取"文化素质+职业技能"的考试方法，职业技能测试以实际操作为主。

业教育、培训和就业，健全终身职业技能培训制度，支持职业学校学生、灵活就业人员、农民工和退役军人等各类学习者通过接受职业教育与培训进一步提升综合素质和就业能力，增强已就业人员的岗位能力，缓解结构性就业矛盾，助力更多劳动者通过自身奋斗跨入中等收入群体。

2. 提升服务城乡融合发展的能力

乡村振兴是共同富裕的必经之路，城乡融合发展是中国式现代化的必然要求。应进一步创新城乡职业教育融合发展机制，优化资源布局，服务新型城镇化建设；进一步扩大职业教育服务面向的群体，关注产业工人、中小企业主以及个体工商户和新型农民等重要群体，以及来自农村和城市低收入家庭学生等弱势群体，助力提升城乡劳动者职业发展和体面就业能力。

3. 扩大终身学习渠道

实现人民群众物质生活和精神生活的共同富裕是中国式现代化的重要特征。应进一步提升职业教育的普惠性，积极满足不同年龄段、不同阶层人群的多样化精神文化需求；依托职业学校基层办学和专业设置全面覆盖国民经济各行业领域的优势，加快建设数字教育基础设施，构建数字平台互联互通机制，扩大优质职业教育数字资源在城乡的覆盖率，丰富课程服务体系，更好地服务个性化学习、终身学习，赋能学习型社会建设。

四、营造职业教育发展的良好生态

职业教育既需要主动对接经济社会发展，也需要社会各界的支持，共同在理念、机制、环境等方面，营造人人皆可成才、人人尽展其才的良好氛围。

1. 在全社会树立正确的成才观

崇尚劳动、尊重劳动者，是中华民族始终如一的美德。应坚持德技并修、知行合一，持续办好职业教育活动周、劳模工匠进校园等品牌活动，进一步弘扬劳动光荣、技能宝贵、创造伟大的时代风尚，激励更多年轻人技能成才、技能报国。

2. 构建政行企校四方协同新格局

校企合作是职业教育的基本办学模式。应进一步构建央地互动、区域联动、多方协同发展职业教育的格局，在国家和省两个层面进一步细化"金融＋财政＋土地＋信用"的激励政策，更好地调动和认可企业作为职业教育重要办学主体的行动和贡献，集聚资金、技术、人才、政策等要素，推动政府、行业、企业、家庭、社会等主体参与职业教育。

3. 畅通技能人才职业发展通道

技能人才是国家战略人才的重要组成。应以更加积极、开放、有效的人才政策，保障职业学校毕业生在落户、就业、参加招录（聘）、职称评聘、晋升等方面与普通学校毕业生享受同等待遇；推行新八级工制度，依据技能水平和创造贡献，提高生产服务一线技能人才工资水平；加大高技能人才表彰奖励力度，激发技能人才干事创业的积极性、主动性和创造性。

五、为构建人类命运共同体贡献力量

职业教育紧密联系经济社会，事关产业发展、民生改善。中国职业教育的成功经验能够为世界提供借鉴，应以更高水平的开放促进共同发展。

1. 积极参与全球职业教育治理

持续深化教育领域多边合作，积极响应联合国教科文组织等国际组织关于全球职业教育发展的理念和倡议，依托区域性和国家间的合作机制以及交流合作平台，向广大发展中国家提供职业教育的技术支持与建设经验，分享中国职业教育数字化转型成果，推动提升全球职业教育治理水平。

2. 主动服务国际产能合作

全球产业链供应链国际合作日益深化，职业教育与产业联动的特性更受关注。应持续推动构建"产教融合、校企协同"的职业教育国际合作机制，继续共建"鲁班工坊"等教育领域"小而美"的民生项目，培育合作新增长点，通过职业教育合作助力全球产业升级与绿色可持续发展，推动国际产能合作，助力所在地国家技能人才培养和高质量就业。

3. 推动构建国际职业教育标准框架

标准是人类文明进步的共同成果，标准促进世界各国互联互通。应探索建立多国参与的合作构架，在多边合作中寻求各方利益的最大公约数，开发符合未来职业技能的职业教育与培训框架，推动跨国技能互认与资历对接，打造稳定、统一、规范的全球职业技术教育环境，推动全球职业教育高质量发展。

第四编　主要举措

2024年是中国教育强国建设的开局之年，职业教育紧紧围绕国家决策部署，以"实实在在把职业教育搞好"的坚定决心和务实行动，规划实施有关行动计划，加快构建职普融通、产教融合的职业教育体系。

一、完善职业教育与普通教育的沟通衔接机制

1. 丰富职业启蒙的载体和路径

构建符合青少年身心发展特点的系统化课程体系和实践教学体系，鼓励职业学校以送课入校、职业讲座、定制课堂、结对导师等形式，支持普通中小学实施职业启蒙教育、劳动教育、职业体验、技能类课程；开展"劳模工匠进校园""优秀职校生校园分享"等活动；在职业学校建设一批中小学职业启蒙、劳动教育实践基地。

2. 拓展横向融通、纵向贯通的学生发展通道

试点建设综合高中等多样化的高中学校，推进中职学校与普通高中之间的师资共享、课程互选、学籍互转、学分互认。支持各省开展中职与高职（3+2）五年贯通、中职与高职本科或应用型本科（3+4）七年贯通、高职专科与高职本科或应用型本科（3+2）五年贯通培养;规范优质中等职业学校与高

等职业学校、应用型本科学校衔接培养模式。吸引普通本科毕业生接受职业教育，实现技能就业。探索终身职业培训新模式与新路径。

3. 优化职教高考等考核评价制度

完善符合职业教育办学规律和技能人才成长规律的考试招生制度，细化"文化素质＋职业技能"的考试招生办法。支持各省因地制宜制定"职教高考"方案，进一步完善职教高考的内容与形式，为学生成长成才提供多样化选择路径；支持国家"双高计划"优质高职专科学校升格成为高职本科学校。鼓励应用型本科院校举办高职本科专业；稳步扩大应用型本科高校和高职本科学校在"职教高考"中的招生规模。

二、完善职业教育与经济和产业发展的匹配机制

1. 建强省域职业教育体系

深化教育部与省级政府协同推进职业教育的发展机制，推动省级政府根据本省实际编制产业发展清单、人才需求清单、政策支持清单，打造推进职业教育改革的具体项目和载体。构建地方职业教育资源与产业布局相匹配的数字地图，指导职业学校在产教融合实践中找准方向、发挥作用。强化各级各类职业学校建设，落实职业学校在内设机构、岗位设置、用人计划、教师招聘、职称评聘等方面的自主权。加大职业教育经费投入力度，建立技能导向的技能人才长效激励机制，实现人力资源的有效供给。

2. 建强市域产教联合体

重点围绕国家7个重大区域发展战略、19个国家级新区、178个国家高新技术产业开发区、229个国家级经济开发区和17个国家级临空经济示范区等经济要素聚集区、产业发展功能区需求，推动地方政府制定规划、出台政策，调

动政府、行业企业、科研机构等各类主体在专业建设、人才培养方案制定、课程教材开发和师资队伍建设等方面与职业学校深度合作；引导学校紧密对接当地产业结构和市场用人需求，优化专业设置，与行业企业联合开展技术攻关，为园区企业提供技术咨询与服务，促进企业技术创新和产品升级；推动各地建强市域产教联合体。在经济发达地区推进职业教育资源下沉到县（市）。

3. 建强行业产教融合共同体

围绕先进制造业、现代农业、现代服务业等重点行业和重点领域，持续建强行业产教融合共同体，成规模、成体系、成建制推动职业学校精准匹配教育资源。以产业链为依托，整合不同区域的产业资源和教育资源，强化不同区域上下游企业的沟通与合作，根据产业链分工对人才类型、层次、结构的要求，推动共同体内学校和企业实行联合招生，通过委托、订单和学徒制等方式，共同培养行业企业所需人才；支持整合校企地方资源建设公共实训基地、高技能人才培训基地、职业技能培训基地，支持终身职业培训。

4. 优化高水平职业学校资源配置

启动新一轮国家层面的示范引导项目，集中力量建设一批高水平高职学校和高水平专业群，重点做好服务地方产业、区域战略、一体两翼、高品质民生、职业教育国际合作等方面的工作；用好评价指挥棒，整体优化设计职业学校资源配置、评价方式、考核机制，引导职业学校由"基础好、条件好"向"服务好、支撑好"转变。

三、扎实推进职业学校教学"新基建"

1. 建设匹配需求、要素集聚的高水平专业

围绕先进制造业集群、数字产业集群等国家重点产业链，梳理分析各环

节、各岗位对技能人才的实际需求，引导职业学校增设与实体经济领域相关专业和新兴紧缺产业相关专业，裁撤过时过剩专业，强化传统专业数字化升级改造，推动专业集群式发展，培养复合型、创新型、发展型的高技能人才；鼓励有条件的职业学校开展托育、护理、康养、家政等民生领域紧缺人才培养，服务普惠性托育、社区嵌入式护理、社区养老等新型机构人才需要。

2. 打造对接岗位、数智融合的一流核心课程

推动职业学校深入行业和企业生产一线，开展人才和职业岗位能力需求调研，推进与关键职业能力联系最为紧密、对高技能人才培养有重要影响的专业核心课程改革，建设职业教育专业教学资源库、精品在线开放课程、一流核心课程、虚拟仿真实训基地等重点项目，打造更多场景课堂，借助数字化、智能化手段推动教育教学与评价方式变革。

3. 开发多元参与、形态多样的产教融合优质教材

依照能力图谱，组织头部企业、高水平职业学校、行业专家共同编写形态多样、反映行业前沿技术的优质教材。将企业生产工艺、技术标准及时转化为教材内容，遴选引入典型任务、生产工单，改造转化企业优质培训教材；加大数字教材开发使用力度，推动数字教材建设率先取得突破，积极发展活页式、工作手册式教材，加强国家规划教材等优质教材的推广使用。

4. 培育结构合理、技艺精湛的"双师型"团队

完善高水平职业教育教师培养培训和企业实践制度，依托龙头企业和高水平高等学校建设国家级"双师型"教师培养培训基地，针对青年教师开展产学研训一体化岗位实践，深入实施职业学校教师学历提升行动、职业学校名师（名匠）名校长培养计划，培育优秀教师团队；鼓励职业学校教师与企业高技能人才按规定互聘兼职；完善职业学校教师绩效工资保障制度。强化教师数字化教学能力培养，提升教师利用数字技术优化、创新和变革教育教学活动的意

识、能力和责任。

5. 建设场景真实、开放融合的高水平专业化实训基地

对标产业发展前沿和生产实景，引导职业学校建设集实践教学、社会培训、真实生产和技术服务功能为一体的开放型区域产教融合实践中心，建设一批公共实践中心、企业实践中心，推动职业学校实训基地数字化、智能化升级；完善学生实习实践制度，基于企业真实生产过程，开发一批在企业生产现场、区域产教融合实践中心或校内生产性实训基地适用的典型生产实践项目，提升学生动手操作、技术成果转化、科技创新等能力。

四、强化育训并举功能

1. 深化产业技术工人培养培训

加强产业工人学历教育和非学历培训，深入实施产业工人"求学圆梦行动"计划，完善高等职业学校单独招生考试制度，全面推行中国特色学徒制培养模式，支持产业工人通过半工半读等形式完成高等教育。实施专业技术人员知识更新工程，发挥好开放型区域产教融合实践中心、公共实训基地、高技能人才培训基地作用，全面实施职业培训促进就业创业行动计划，广泛开展数字技能岗前培训、在岗培训和转岗转业培训等，提高产业工人数字技能。

2. 深化高素质农民培养培训

加强市级政府统筹，集中力量办好县域职业教育中心，整合职业技能培训项目和资金，大力支持举办涉农职业教育专业，打造精准服务乡村振兴的特色专业群；以定向招生、定向培养、定向就业方式深入实施"一村一名大学生"计划，大力开展农村劳动力转移培训、农村实用技术培训、农村基层干部素质提高培训，加快培养农村科技骨干和致富带头人，为乡村振兴提供

人才和技能支撑。

3. 深化社区居民培训

建设县域社区学习中心，构建泛在可及的终身教育体系和制度框架，打造"15分钟学习圈"，通过教育微课、线上社区大讲堂、市民夜校等线上线下相结合的多样化学习形式，为社区居民提供生产生活技能体验、技能学习公共服务。加强社区老年大学建设，建立资源共建共享网络，开发老年人喜闻乐见的课程，为社会大众提供文化创意、非遗传承、传统手工艺、职业技能、生活技能和兴趣类课程。

五、推进职业教育数字化

1. 迭代升级国家职业教育智慧教育平台

将智能技术与职业教育教学深度融合，丰富完善平台功能，全覆盖、个性化服务学生学、教师教和教学管。聚焦以智助学，开发智能学伴、实施智能辅导，探索开展AI客服不间断在线答疑，为学习者提供一站式、全方位、全过程学习支持服务；聚焦以智助教，研发智能助教，支撑教师备授课，为教师工作减负增效，让教师有更多精力去从事创造性教学活动、育人活动；聚焦以智助管，开发智能作业、互动课堂、线上教研、辅助阅卷和教育评价等数字教育工具和平台。

2. 开发汇聚高质量数字学习资源

采取师生自主创造、学校自主建设、政府统筹征集等方式，着力增加专业课程、美育课程和劳动教育课程资源，持续推动职业教育专业教学资源库、精品在线开放课程等重点项目建设，不断扩大职业教育资源供给。大力开发数字教材，广泛集纳教辅、教案、课件、教学设计、虚拟仿真实训资源，不断丰富职业教育资源形态。创新资源评价方式，运用国家教育大数据中心集聚的动态数据，对平台资源规模、结构、内容及使用效果等分类分析评价，推进职业教育资源开发、入库、更新、出库的全生命周期管理。

3. 开展大规模职业教育数字化应用示范行动

着力推进国家职业教育智慧教育平台全域、全员、全过程应用，扩大优质资源覆盖面，推动试点转示范。鼓励职业学校将平台资源和智能化服务嵌入教育教学，用数字教育资源丰富拓展学生的第二课堂，支持发展学生的兴趣爱好；大力推进职业学校智慧校园建设，主动适应学习方式变革，探索数字赋能大规模因材施教、创新性教学与个性化教学；完善国家职业教育智慧教育平台国际版，分区域、分国别、分语种服务全球学习者。

六、开展高水平国际交流合作

1. 搭建更具韧性的世界职业教育交流舞台

搭建好"中国–东盟职业教育发展大会""中国–亚欧博览会·教育国际论坛""未来非洲——中非职业教育合作计划""金砖国家职业教育联盟"等平台，完善职业教育国际交流合作机制。高标准、高水平举办世界职业技术教育发展大会，组建世界职业教育联盟、设立世界职业教育大奖及世界职业技术教育展等。

2. 打造更具国际性的职业学校技能大赛

持续优化世界职业院校技能大赛，优化赛道设置；调整完善比赛内容和形式，围绕生产管理服务一线的实际需求设计比赛项目。紧扣全面考核学生综合能力、综合技能目标设计比赛形式，增设与国际接轨的竞赛项目，扩大参赛范围，加强与国际职业教育机构、世界技能大赛组织机构的交流合作。

3. 塑造职业教育国际交流品牌

推进职业教育国际化发展，提升职业学校国际合作能力，建设"中文＋职业技能"培训基地，培养国际化人才和中资企业急需的本土技能人才；持续推进"鲁班工坊""丝路学院""中文工坊"等品牌项目，产教融合、校企协同推进国际合作，优化项目运行、项目准入、质量监控及退出机制。

4. 共建共享职业教育标准

推动职业学校依托实质运行的国际职业教育合作项目，与行业企业共同研制基础良好、业内领先、具有较高国际认可度的专业教学标准、课程标准和实习实训标准等，推动相关标准在国内外职业学校的落地实施。

Preface

The development of vocational education in China has a long and storied history, characterized by its vital contributions to the history of global civilization and education. In light of the various challenges and opportunities arising in its current economy, society, population, environment, and employment, China expedited the development of its modern vocational education, which has resulted in a series of notable achievements, including effectively bolstering the high-quality development of the nation's economy and society, continuously meeting the public's aspirations for a better living quality, nurturing diverse student growth and talent development, and actively contributing to the creation of a comprehensive and open new framework for global engagement. China's vocational education sector has undergone unprecedented and inspiring transformations in scope, depth, scale, and quality.

In 2023, China's gross enrollment rate for senior high school education reached 91.80%, with students in secondary vocational education accounting for nearly 40% of the total in this stage, helping the overall level of basic education reach an upper-middle standard globally. Annual enrollment in higher vocational education exceeded that in general undergraduate programs, pushing the gross enrollment rate for higher education past 60%, marking a historic leap and moving higher education into the globally recognized stage of universal access. These developments also demonstrate vocational education's outstanding performance in China's educational reforms and reflect its significance in the development of vocational education worldwide.

China leverages vocational education to support national development, inherit Chinese civilization, and promote craftsmanship spirit. It continues to advance the integration of industry and education, effective school-enterprise co-operation, and the development of a skilled society. The country has established the world's largest vocational education system, creating a government-led, school-centered vocational education model integrating industry and education. This model provides a key platform for equitable growth and lifelong develop-ment for skilled talents, making vocational education a vital force in supporting China's growth from a major manufacturing nation to a manufacturing power-house.

Today's world is undergoing profound changes unseen in a century, with markedly heightened instability and uncertainty. Vocational education needs to be given greater priority in response to the ever-changing world and dynamics, as well as to adapt to the new challenges brought by technological and digital revolutions and industry transformation. It must be woven into the development strategy to promote its synchrony with the needs of the economy and society, providing solid support for the global industrial and service markets with skilled talents. As China enters a deeper stage of comprehensive and deepened reforms to promote Chinese-style modernization, the nation will make coordinated ef-forts to promote integrated development of education, science and technology, and talent, aiming to establish itself as a leading education power by 2035. China is committed to empowering the building of a community with a shared future for humanity through vocational education. It seeks to collaborate with coun-tries worldwide with more open concepts, standards, resources, and mechanisms to explore new paths and models in vocational education development, jointly address global development challenges, enhance people's welfare, and promote sustainable global development.

The *Report on the Development of Vocational Education in China* focuses on the sector's achievements, experience, strategic tasks, and primary measures, supported by a wealth of facts, data, and case studies. It aims to provide a panoramic view of the Chinese vocational education sector's practical experiences and innovative successes in system development and refinement, industry-education integration, quality enhancement, and international cooperation since 2012. This demonstrates the vitality and robust momentum of China's vocational education development. With a forward-looking perspective, it outlines a blueprint and strategic tasks for vocational education in the new era, providing reference and inspiration for the continued prosperity of China's vocational education and the development of global vocational education.

Chapter One: Achievements

China places great importance on vocational education development, viewing it as an essential part of the national education system and human resource development. Vocational education is tasked with nurturing diverse talents, preserving skills, and promoting employment and entrepreneurship. Since 2012, vocational education in China has achieved historic progress in scale, system, model, quality, and international cooperation, undergoing structural changes and becoming the primary platform for training highly skilled talents, as well as outstanding artisans and Craftsmen of the Nation.

I. Creating the World's Largest Vocational Education System

The government coordinates and consolidates resources from all sectors, integrating vocational and general education and combining education and training. This has led to a vocational education system that adapts to social and economic development and supports lifelong learning for all. Vocational schools produce over 10 million graduates annually and provide vocational training for approximately 13 million people each year. Over 70% of new front-line workers in modern manufacturing, strategic emerging industries, and modern services are graduates of vocational schools.

(I) Forming a Well-Structured Training System

1. Complete Vocational School Structure Making Vocational Schools the Primary Source of Talent Supply

Vocational schools are categorized into a structure comprising secondary vocational education, higher vocational education (associate degree), and higher vocational education (bachelor's degree). The prominence of higher vocational education (associate degree) has grown significantly, while higher vocational education (bachelor's degree) has also seen steady development (Fig. 1–1).

In 2023, China had 11,133 vocational schools, including 9,553 secondary vocational schools[1], 1,547 associate-degree higher vocational schools, and 33 bachelor's degree higher vocational schools. Since 2012, the number of secondary

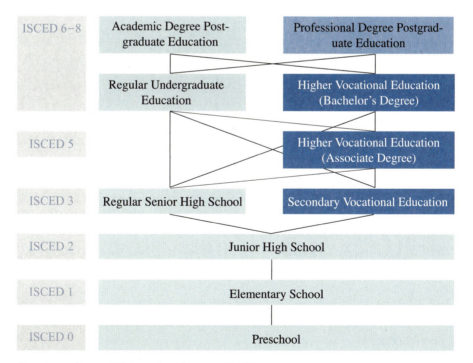

Fig. 1–1: Current Education System in China

---

1   Technical schools included.

vocational schools has been gradually decreasing, while the number of higher vocational schools has shown steady growth (Fig. 1–2).

Vocational school graduates have become a key source of new urban labor force and first-class industrial technicians. In 2023, vocational schools approximately had 34.78 million students enrolled, with approximately 17.38 million in secondary vocational and approximately 17.40 million in higher vocational education, including bachelor's degree programs (Fig. 1–3). In 2022, vocational education graduates neally reached 10 million, reaching 10.94 million in 2023 (Fig. 1–4). The proportion of higher vocational graduates in new urban employment has steadily increased, reaching 31.79% in 2020, 41.04% in 2022, and 44.77% in 2023, respectively (Fig. 1–5).

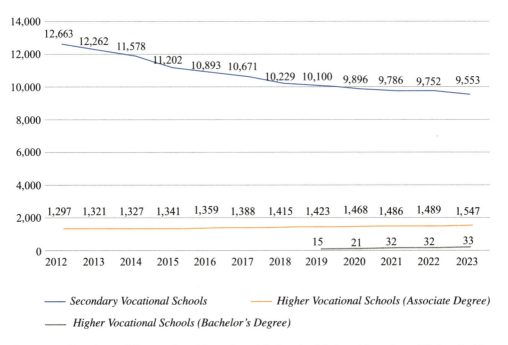

Fig. 1–2: Number of Secondary Vocational Schools, Higher Vocational Schools (Associate Degree), and Higher Vocational Schools (Bachelor's Degree) from 2012 to 2023 (in 10,000s) [1]

---

[1]   Source: National Education Development Statistical Bulletin (2012—2023); Human Resources and Social Security Development Statistical Bulletin (2012—2023).

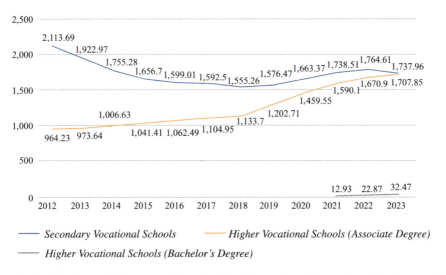

Fig. 1-3: Number of Students Enrolled in Secondary Vocational Schools, Higher Vocational Schools (Associate Degree), and Higher Vocational Schools (Bachelor's Degree) from 2012 to 2023 (in 10,000s) [1]

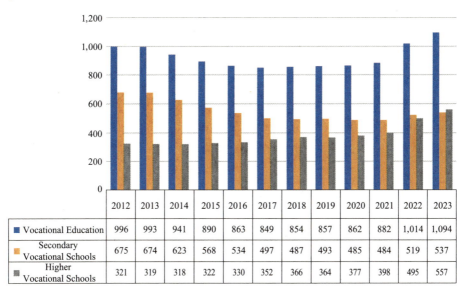

	2012	2013	2014	2015	2016	2017	2018	2019	2020	2021	2022	2023
■ Vocational Education	996	993	941	890	863	849	854	857	862	882	1,014	1,094
■ Secondary Vocational Schools	675	674	623	568	534	497	487	493	485	484	519	537
■ Higher Vocational Schools	321	319	318	322	330	352	366	364	377	398	495	557

Fig. 1-4: Number of Graduates from Vocational Education, Secondary Vocational Schools, and Higher Vocational Schools (Associate and Bachelor's Degree) from 2012 to 2023 (in 10,000s) [2]

---

1   Source: National Education Development Statistical Bulletin (2012—2023); Human Resources and Social Security Development Statistical Bulletin (2012—2023).

2   Source: National Education Development Statistical Bulletin (2012—2023); Human Resources and Social Security Development Statistical Bulletin (2012—2023).

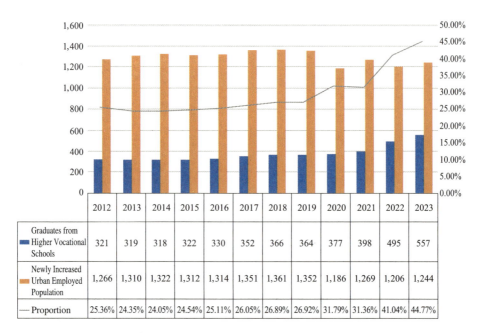

	2012	2013	2014	2015	2016	2017	2018	2019	2020	2021	2022	2023
Graduates from Higher Vocational Schools	321	319	318	322	330	352	366	364	377	398	495	557
Newly Increased Urban Employed Population	1,266	1,310	1,322	1,312	1,314	1,351	1,361	1,352	1,186	1,269	1,206	1,244
Proportion	25.36%	24.35%	24.05%	24.54%	25.11%	26.05%	26.89%	26.92%	31.79%	31.36%	41.04%	44.77%

Fig. 1-5: Changes in the Scale and Proportion of Graduates from Vocational Colleges (Including Bachelor's Degree) and Newly Increased Urban Employed Population from 2012 to 2023 (in 10,000s) [1]

The number of vocational school teachers has steadily increased, and their structure has been further optimized. The total number of full-time vocational school teachers grew from 1.30 million in 2012 to 1.45 million in 2023 (Fig. 1-6); part-time teachers have also expanded, reaching 253,700 in 2023, an increase of 9.40% from the previous year, including over 8,000 *Craftsmen of the Nation* and *Model Workers*, with industry mentors delivering a total of 428 million class hours per year.

2. Vertical Integration Within Vocational Education, Horizontal Integration with General Education

The connection channels within vocational education and between vocational

---

1   Source: National Education Development Statistical Bulletin (2012—2023). Data from 2021 to 2023 does not include technical schools.

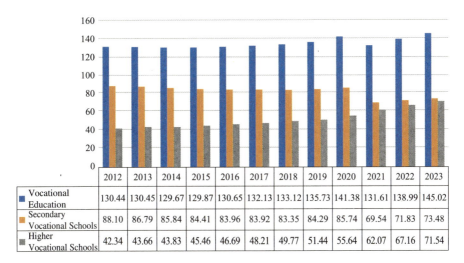

	2012	2013	2014	2015	2016	2017	2018	2019	2020	2021	2022	2023
■ Vocational Education	130.44	130.45	129.67	129.87	130.65	132.13	133.12	135.73	141.38	131.61	138.99	145.02
■ Secondary Vocational Schools	88.10	86.79	85.84	84.41	83.96	83.92	83.35	84.29	85.74	69.54	71.83	73.48
■ Higher Vocational Schools	42.34	43.66	43.83	45.46	46.69	48.21	49.77	51.44	55.64	62.07	67.16	71.54

Fig. 1−6: Number of Full-Time Teachers in Secondary Vocational and Higher Vocational Schools from 2012 to 2023 in Vocational Education (in 10,000s) [1]

education and general higher education provides students with more options for their development. Starting in 2014, China separated higher vocational entrance exams from the general college entrance exams, mainly implementing the "Academic Competence + Vocational Skills" assessment model by province. The scale of admissions through the categorized vocational entrance exams has since expanded annually, becoming the main channel for higher vocational schools to recruit students from both secondary vocational schools and regular senior high schools. Additionally, multiple pathway options, such as five-year integrated model of higher vocational programs, three-year secondary + two-year higher vocational programs, and three-year higher vocational + two-year bachelor's programs, offer students diverse development choices. In 2023 alone, 607,000 students transitioned from secondary to higher vocational education through the five-year programs, accounting for 10.94% [2] of that year's higher vocational

1   Source: National Education Development Statistical Bulletin (2012—2023). Data from 2021 to 2023 does not include technical schools.

2   Source: 2023 National Education Development Statistical Bulletin.

associate-degree admissions. Approximately 20% of associate-degree higher vocational graduates advance to bachelor's degree programs annually through the "top-up" examination [1].

The integration of vocational and general education has increasingly shown positive results. Over the past decade, over 4,500 vocational schools have supported nearly 110,000 primary and secondary schools in implementing labor education practices and vocational enlightenment education, influencing over 15 million participating students to embrace the ideals of serving the country through skills and achieving personal success through skills. Some regions have proactively explored mutual exchanges of teachers, resources, courses, and credit recognition between secondary vocational schools and regular senior high schools.

3. Equal Emphasis on School Education and Vocational Training

China is actively pushing a lifelong vocational skills training system. The central government is implementing measures to enhance vocational skills by supporting vocational schools with subsidized training and expanding programs tailored for workers, key employment groups, and economically disadvantaged labor forces. In the past five years, government-subsidized training has reached an average of nearly 24 million individuals annually. The Ministry of Education, in collaboration with the All-China Federation of Trade Unions, has launched the "Fulfilling Dreams of Pursuing Education" initiative, which has successfully assisted over 2.4 million front-line workers in improving their educational qualifications. Furthermore, there have been over 10 million instances of participation in relevant vocational training sessions.

---

1   Students pass the examination and then will be promoted from higher vocational colleges to undergraduate universities. This kind of examination is led by provincial educational administrative departments and organized by Provincial Academy of Education and Examination in each province.

(II) Facilitating a Well-Coordinated Management System for Vocational Education

1. Building a Series of Legal Institutions

China highly prioritizes the legislation of vocational education. At the national level, the *Vocational Education Law of the People's Republic of China* was promulgated and implemented in 1996, marking the entry of vocational education development into a legal framework. The Vocational Education Law was revised in 2022, consolidating the fundamental experiences and institutional achievements of more than two decades of extensive development in vocational education. At the local level, some provinces and municipalities have planned and promulgated local vocational education regulations and corresponding enforcement inspection systems based on their specific needs, further enhancing the legal framework governing vocational education. Since 2022, provinces such as Anhui, Tianjin, Shandong, and Sichuan have enacted local vocational education regulations. Provinces including Hunan, Henan, Liaoning, and Shanxi are currently soliciting public opinions, and cities like Qingdao, Wuxi, Shenzhen, and Guangzhou have included the formulation or amendment of regulations in their legislative plans. Tianjin has implemented the *Tianjin Regulations on Promoting Industry-Education Integration in Vocational Education*. At the same time, Jiangsu Province, Jilin Province, Quzhou city, Ningbo city, Taizhou city, and the Ili Kazakh Autonomous Prefecture have introduced local regulations to promote cooperation between schools and enterprises.

2. Clarifying the Division of Responsibilities in Macro-Management

The State Council serves as the national coordinator for vocational education affairs. The Ministry of Education is responsible for planning, coordinating, and macro-managing vocational education. The Ministry of Education, the

Ministry of Human Resources and Social Security, and other relevant industry regulatory departments fulfill their responsibilities pertinent to vocational education within the scope defined by the State Council. In alignment with the needs of economic and social development, the Ministry of Education, in collaboration with relevant authorities, organizes the development and revision of vocational education major program catalogs, improves vocational education standards, and oversees the approval and filing of vocational schools and majors, as well as manages and guides the formulation of textbooks. The Ministry of Human Resources and Social Security is tasked with establishing a coordinated system for occupational skills training both in urban and rural area, improving the vocational qualification system, the occupational classification system, and industry-specific vocational skill standards.

3. Building a Refined Tiered Management System

Vocational education management authorities are established at the national, provincial, and municipal levels, ensuring the implementation of national vocational education policies through a tiered management system. Provincial governments are authorized by law to consolidate and optimize the responsibilities of vocational education within municipalities and counties, centralizing the management of vocational education's development across the province. Local governments at all levels, within the policy boundaries set by the central government, formulate policies and measures tailored to local conditions to promote the development of vocational education locally while guiding and supervising vocational education locally.

(III) Building a Diverse and Coordinated System of Supporting Services

1. Establishing Specialized Support Institutions

In 2022, built upon the foundation of Central Institute for Vocational and Technical Education, Ministry of Education, P.R.China (CIVTE), Center for Vocational Education Development, Ministry of Education, P.R.China (CVED) was established. This center provides support for the Ministry of Education in formulating vocational education policies and implementing projects. It also offers public services to the society and is committed to be a capacity building platform, a collaborative innovation platform, an exchange and cooperation platform, and a publicity and promotion platform for vocational education.

2. Forming a Professional Research System

In terms of institutions, national and local educational research institutions, represented by the Chinese National Academy of Educational Sciences, all have established dedicated departments or positions for vocational education research. Some higher vocational schools have also set up specialized institutions to conduct educational and teaching research in vocational education. In terms of disciplines, represented by Beijing Normal University and East China Normal University, over 50 institutions of higher education nationwide, have established vocational and technical education disciplines. They are engaging in cultivating top-level research-oriented talents in the field of vocational education, as well as in discipline development and research. In terms of publications, four core Chinese journals, such as *Chinese Vocational and Technical Education,* the English-language journal *Vocation, Technology & Education*, and over 20 professional academic journals and 164 journals hosted by vocational schools, serve as carriers to promote and exchange research findings in vocational education.

3. Enabling Collaborative Support from Various Organizations

All sectors of society participate in supporting vocational education in various forms. The China Vocational Education Association extensively connects with people in vocational education and private education sectors both at home and abroad, to promote, research and couduct vocational education. The All-China Federation of Trade Unions, using union organizations as the main platform, promotes skill improvement among industrial workers and drives technological innovation. The Chinese Society for Technical and Vocational Education, a national and academic social organization, plays a significant role as a think tank. The China Education Association for International Exchange actively promotes civil exchanges and cooperation in vocational education between China and other countries/regions. The Ministry of Education has facilitated the establishment of 57 sector-specific vocational education teaching advisory boards, and 6 teaching (education) guidance committees for vocational schools, providing consultation and guidance services for vocational education and training in related industries.

4. Refining the System for Skills Competitions

The National Vocational College Skills Competition has been held continuously for 16 years, and has been comprehensively upgraded to the World Vocational College Skills Competition in 2024; since 2020, China has held the National Vocational Skills Competition biennially. These competitions have spurred a wave of professional competitions across industries, local areas, enterprises, and colleges. A skills competition system has been established, which takes school-level competitions as the foundation, provincial-level competitions as the main body and world-level competitions as the guide, with seamless connections both vertically and horizontally. This system has promoted the specialty construction and reform of vocational education. China has participated in the WorldSkills Competition for seven consecutive sessions, and its achievements have been steadily improved. At the 47th WorldSkills Competition, which concluded in September 2024, China competed in all 59 competitions, winning 36 gold medals, 9 silver medals, 4 bronze medals, and 8 medallions of excellence, leading in gold medals, overall medals, and team scores. Of the 66 award-winning competitors, 59 were from vocational schools.

5. Celebrating Vocational Education Week

Since 2015, the State Council has designated the second week of May each year as Vocational Education Week. Across departments nationwide, concentrated publicity has been carried out on laws and regulations, guiding principles and policies, construction achievements, societal impacts, reform experiences, and outstanding figures related to vocational education. Over the years, 74,500 vocational schools, more than 100 million students, 30,000 enterprises, and 130 million individuals from all walks of life have participated in Vocational Education Weeks, which has immensely promoted the fashion of the times that glorifies labor, values skills and honors creativity throughout the whole society, fostering a positive public mentality that respects practical skills over academic credentials alone.

II. Establishing a Vocational Education Development Model with Chinese Characteristics

Over years of in-field practice, China has gradually developed a vocational education model characterized by "government leading, schools as the main body, and the integration of industry and education." In 2022, *Opinions on Deepening the Reform of the Modern Vocational Education System Construction* released by the General Office of the Central Committee of the Communist Party of China and the General Office of the State Council, put forward new reform measures known as *"One Body, Two Wings, Five Key Points."* These reforms aim to establish a coordination mechanism between central and provincial governments. A new reform mechanism was designed for reforms in vocational education, driven by central-local communication, inter-regional collaboration, and coordinated efforts among government, industries, enterprises, and educational institutions. The focus is on creating a new ecosystem for vocational education development that ensures ample institutional supply, strong condition guarantee, and in-depth industry-education integration.

(I) Exploring New Models for Provincial Modern Vocational Education System

The "One Body" refers to exploring new models for the provincial modern vocational education system. The Ministry of Education, in line with national and regional development planning and major strategies, has selected provinces (autonomous regions, municipalities) with necessary conditions, willingness for reform, and mature designs to pilot these initiatives. The industry-education integration, as well as the integration of vocational and general education, will serve as part of the reform direction, optimizing the institutional environment and ecosystems for the development of local vocational education. These efforts are expected to provide new, replicable cases and models with broad application potential and drive broader quality improvements across the system.

In 2023, the Ministry of Education established new models for provincial modern vocational education systems jointly with eight provinces, autonomous regions, and municipalities (Guangxi Zhuang Autonomous Region, Tianjin Municipality, Shandong Province, Xinjiang Uygur Autonomous Region, Heilongjiang Province, Zhejiang Province, Chongqing Municipality, and Hunan

Province). Based on the specific local conditions and tasks, each of these local governments released its implementation plan for provincial modern vocational education system construction and reforms (Table 1-1). These plans aim to innovate and reform the vocational education system and mechanisms, creating local development models for modern vocational education that match the local industrial structure and align with regional development with distinctive local characteristics, thus making vocational education better positioned to serve regional economic and social development.

Table 1-1: 8 Implementation Plans for Provincial Modern Vocational Education System Construction and Reforms

No.	Provinces (Autonomous Regions, and Municipalities)	Title of Documents Jointly Issued by Ministry of Education and Provincial Governments	Issuance Date
1	Guangxi	Implementation Plan for Promoting the Agglomeration and Integration of Industry and Education and Building an Innovative Highland for Vocational Education Open-Cooperation Facing ASEAN	April 19, 2023
2	Tianjin	Implementation Plan for Exploring New Models of the Construction and Reform of the Modern Vocational Education System	May 8, 2023
3	Shandong	Implementation Opinions on Promoting the Quality Improvement and Upgrading of Vocational Education to Empower the Construction of a Green, Low-Carbon and High-Quality Development Pilot Zone	May 19, 2023
4	Xinjiang	Implementation Opinions on Deepening the Construction and Reform of the Modern Vocational Education System	July 13, 2023
5	Heilongjiang	Implementation Plan for Promoting the Integration of Vocational Education and Industrial Cluster Agglomeration to Revitalize Development in Longjiang	October 18, 2023
6	Zhejiang	Implementation Plan for Accelerating the Upgrading and Empowerment of Vocational Education to Empower the Construction of a Demonstration Zone for Common Prosperity	November 28, 2023

continued Table

No.	Provinces (Autonomous Regions, and Municipalities)	Title of Documents Jointly Issued by Ministry of Education and Provincial Governments	Issuance Date
7	Chongqing	Implementation Plan for Deepening the Reform of the Modern Vocational Education System to Serve the Construction of the Chengdu-Chongqing Economic Circle	December 27, 2023
8	Hunan	Implementation Plan for Further Deepening the Integration of Vocational Education and Industry to Serve the Construction of an Important and Advanced Manufacturing Highland of the Country	December 29, 2023

(II) Constructing Municipal Industry-Education Consortia and Sector-Specific Industry-Education Integration Communities

"Two Wings" refer to the municipal industry-education consortia and industry-education integration communities. The Ministry of Education supports provincial and municipal governments to create these consortia on the basis of industrial parks, in partnership with industries, enterprises, and educational institutions, with equal emphasis on talent training, innovation and entrepreneurship, and promoting high-quality industrial economic development. Their goal is to drive in-depth participation in vocational education from various entities. In critical industries and sectors, supports leading enterprises along with general and vocational schools are supported to lead the formation of industry-education integration groups involving schools, research institutions, and upstream and downstream enterprises, providing stable human resources and technical support to the industry.

In 2023, the Ministry of Education selected and founded the first 28 municipal industry-education consortia nationwide, and in 2024, six new ones have been founded, ultimately leading to the establishment of 237 provincial and municipal industry-education consortia, reinforcing the "closeness" of the combination between vocational education and local economies. In July 2023 and July 2024, two national industry-education integration communities were established in the national rail-transit equipment industry and the national non-ferrous metal industries, driving the construction of more than 1,100 industry-education integration communities across various sectors and enhancing the "adaptability" of vocational education to the needs of industry development. The two national communities have worked together to mobilize general schools, vocational schools, and enterprises to build teaching teams and co-create teaching resources, putting an emphasis on developing 80 majors, creating 270 core professional courses and 330 high-quality textbooks, and establishing 200 production practice centers and 280 productive training projects.

(III) Enhancing Key School-Running Capacities

To tackle the critical challenges in reforming and developing vocational education, the Ministry of Education is dedicated to enhancing the key school-running capacities of vocational schools in areas such as standards, majors, courses, textbooks, teachers, and the construction of training bases. These efforts have resulted in a series of impressive achievements (Table 1–2).

Table 1–2: Achievements of Vocational Schools in Enhancing Key School-Running Capacities

Category	Item	Result
National Standard System	School Standards	8
	Major Outlines	1,349
	Teaching Standards of Majors	987
	Curriculum Standards for General Basic Courses in Secondary Vocational Schools	10
	Internship Standards at the Workplace	151
	Teacher Standards	5

continued Table

Category	Item	Result
High-level Schools	High-level Vocational Schools with Chinese Characteristics	197
	High-quality Secondary Vocational Schools	2,121
High-level Majors / Clusters of Majors	High-level Vocational Majors / Clusters of Majors	253
	High-quality Secondary Vocational Majors	4,198
High-level Courses	National High-quality Online Courses	1,160
	National Professional Teaching Resource Databases for Vocational Education	203
High-quality Textbooks	The First Batch of National Vocational Education Textbooks for the "14th Five Year Plan" period	7,251
	Outstanding Textbooks Winning the National Textbook Construction Award	315
Highly Skilled "Double-Qualified" Teachers	National Vocational Education Teacher Innovation Team	511
	New Era Training Program for Renowned Teachers (Craftsmen) and Principals	260
	"Double-Qualified" Teachers Training Bases and Principals Training Bases	213
	National Vocational Education Teacher Enterprise Practice Bases	202
Industry-Education Integration Practice Centers	Public Training Bases for Supporting Local Construction	327

1. Establishing a National Standard System with a "Trinity" Structure

The Ministry of Education takes the lead and works with relevant departments to draft and develop national vocational education standards. This initiative has formed a national vocational education standard system that includes three sets of standards, namely school vocational education standards, teaching standards, and teacher standards, which sets baseline for enhancing the key school-running capacities of vocational schools. Moreover, eight tiered and categorized standards have been established for vocational schools, including the

Trial Standards for Undergraduate Vocational Schools and the *Standards for the Establishment of Secondary Vocational Schools for the Disabled*, guiding the operations of vocational institutions. Closely aligning with industry standards, vocational standards and post standards, the Ministry of Education has engaged with industry organizations, key enterprises, and research institutions to formulate and release 1,349 major outlines, 987 teaching standards of majors, 10 curriculum standards for general basic courses in secondary vocational schools, 151 internship standards, and four currently implemented teacher standards. Building upon this framework, Shandong Province has crafted 322 teaching standards of majors and 147 curriculum standards that connect secondary vocational education, higher vocational education and applied undergraduate education. Jiangsu Province has developed 106 instructional vocational talent training plans and created 520 curriculum standards for core courses of 5-year higher vocational programs (Fig. 1–7).

2. Developing High-Level Vocational Schools and Majors (Clusters)

As for higher vocational education, in 2019, the Ministry of Education identified 197 national high-level higher vocational schools and 253 high-level major clusters (hereinafter referred to as the "Double High-Level Plan"). This initiative facilitated the establishment of 823 provincial high-level vocational schools and 1,876 high-level major clusters. In the area of secondary vocational education, nearly 1,000 national demonstration schools were created to advance vocational education reform and development, and alongside an additional 2,000 schools have met the construction standards for provincial backbone schools, with the high-quality resources of both national and provincial demonstration schools currently serving over 50% of enrolled students. Relying on high-level schools and majors, China has effectively trained many highly skilled professionals in critical demand across various industries. This initiative is vital in supporting national

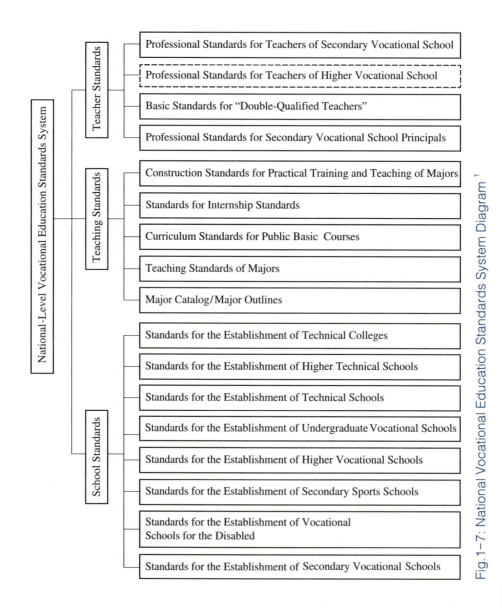

	Professional Standards for Teachers of Secondary Vocational School
	Professional Standards for Teachers of Higher Vocational School
Teacher Standards	Basic Standards for "Double-Qualified Teachers"
	Professional Standards for Secondary Vocational School Principals

	Construction Standards for Practical Training and Teaching of Majors
	Standards for Internship Standards
Teaching Standards	Curriculum Standards for Public Basic Courses
	Teaching Standards of Majors
	Major Catalog/Major Outlines

	Standards for the Establishment of Technical Colleges
	Standards for the Establishment of Higher Technical Schools
	Standards for the Establishment of Technical Schools
School Standards	Standards for the Establishment of Undergraduate Vocational Schools
	Standards for the Establishment of Higher Vocational Schools
	Standards for the Establishment of Secondary Sports Schools
	Standards for the Establishment of Vocational Schools for the Disabled
	Standards for the Establishment of Secondary Vocational Schools

National-Level Vocational Education Standards System

Fig.1–7: National Vocational Education Standards System Diagram [1]

1   Professional Standards for Teachers of Higher Vocational School are currently under development.

and regional development strategies, driving industrial progress, and fostering technological innovation within enterprises. Over the past five years, the "Double High-Level Plan" has recevied a fund of 10.626 billion *yuan* from the central government, which has, in turn, attracted an additional 63.891 billion *yuan* from local governments, sponsors, enterprises, and schools. Consequently, the participating schools have experienced significant enhancements in their campus infrastructure and a marked improvement in educational quality, with notable performance gains in projects funded by the central government.

3. Developing High-Quality Courses and Textbooks

A total of 1,160 national high-quality online courses and 203 national teaching resource databases for vocational majors have been established. The first group of textbooks drafted under the national vocational education textbooks planned for the "14th Five-Year Plan" period comprises 7,251 titles, with 315 vocational education textbooks winning the National Textbook Construction Award. National Vocational Education of Smart Education Platform has been launched online, providing access to more than 7.15 million high-quality teaching resources, which include 1,777 virtual simulation resources, 10,389 high-quality online courses, and 1,559 teaching resource databases for vocational majors. This platform currently serves over1,500 higher vocational colleges, over 3,000 secondary vocational schools, and 3,200 enterprises and organizations, benefitting over 23 million individuals and achieving a total number of views over 4.5 billion times.

4. Cultivating a Group of High-Level "Double-Qualified" Teachers

High-level colleges, leading companies, and vocational schools have joined hands to build 213 "Double-Qualified" teacher training bases and principal training bases, 202 national vocational education teacher enterprise practice bases have released 1,792 teacher practice projects and provided more than 20,000 practice positions. The Plan for Improving the Quality of Vocational School Teachers has successfully conducted national training for 136,000 participants and provincial training for 92,000 participants, along with 80 national vocational education training demonstration projects. Implemented in three stages, 511 national vocational education teacher innovation teams have been built, covering all provincial-level educational administrative units. The "New Era Training Program for Renowned Teachers (Craftsmen) and Principals of Vocational Schools" has been launched and implemented, with more than 260 teachers identified as the first batch of trainees. The proportion of full-time "Double-Qualified" teachers in secondary vocational education across the nation reached 56.71% [1] in 2023.

5. Founding Open Regional Industry-Education Integration Practice Centers

By the end of 2023, 327 local public training bases have been successfully founded, with a cumulative total of nearly 3 million person-times of training. For example, with government leadership and diverse investment support, Shandong Province established a large-scale regional open industry-education integration practice center in each of its 16 cities, along with 194 sub-centers, each serving specialized functions, creating a practice base system characterized by technological leadership and effective resource sharing. In a similar fashion, Jiangxi Province developed 52 regional industry-education integration practice centers alongside 27 vocational education virtual simulation demonstration training bases.

---

1   Source: National Education Development Statistical Bulletin (2023).

III. Continuously Improving the Ability to Cultivate High-Quality Talents

To meet the heightened demands for skilled talent training required by the modern industrial system, China remains committed to fostering virtue through education, and innovating in talent training models, consistently enhancing its competency and quality of talent development.

(I) Refining Mechanisms for Moral and Technical Education

1. Deepening the Integration of Moral Education

Ideals, moral values, and the spirit of craftsmen are organically incorporated throughout the process of professional knowledge acquisition and skill training. The initiative has launched 200 ideological-political demonstration courses in vocational education and 11 teaching and research demonstration centers; nearly 400,000 vocational school educators around the nation have participated in the collective lesson preparation for curriculum-based ideological and political education, reinforcing students' ideological, political, moral, and vocational ethics, and effectively enhancing public morals, family virtues, and personal morality.

2. Consistently Enriching Educational Activities

For 21 consecutive years, the "Grace of Civilization" initiative has significantly contributed to enhancing students' ideological and moral quality and overall quality. Since 2022, China has continued a series of initiatives, including activities to pass on excellent traditional Chinese culture through skills, the "Future Craftsmen" reading campaign, and the "Model Craftsmen Entering Campus" initiative, the "Skills for Success, My Contribution to a Strong Nation" program and so on. These activities have collectively attracted over 50 million student visits each year, making "Skills for Success, Skills for the Nation" a consensus.

3. Consistently Promoting the "3-in-1" Educational Approach

Adherence to the "full-involvement, full-process, and full-dimension" educational approach ensures a comprehensive political and moral education coverage without interruptions. This approach seeks to help students consistently adopt and practice core socialist values, enabling them to develop healthy personalities and noble characters. Over 3,100 class advisor studios have been founded, with more than 50,000 teachers participating in workshops, giving play to the main role of head teachers in secondary vocational schools in educating students through management.

(II) Refining the Vocational Teaching Systems That Align with Industry Needs

1. Revising Major Catalog Based on Industry Demands

In 2021, the Ministry of Education conducted a comprehensive revision of the vocational major catalog, integrating the structure and interrelationships of secondary vocational education, associate-degree higher vocational education, and bachelor's degree higher vocational education. The updated catalog comprises 19 categories, 97 sub-categories, and a total of 1,349 majors, including 358 at the secondary level, 744 at the associate degree level, and 247 at the bachelor's degree level (Fig.1–8). The new catalog focuses on strategic emerging industries, the modern service sector, digital transformation, and rural revitalization. The majors in this catalog encompasses all sectors of the national economy, aligning closely with the distribution of the three economic sectors, which were 4.20% from the primary sector, 38.70% from the secondary sector, and 57.10% from the tertiary sector. In the meantime, the structure of majors in the catalog essentially matches the development trends and contributions of the three sectors to GDP in 2021, which were 7.30% from the primary sector, 39.40% from the secondary sector, and 53.30% from the tertiary sector. (Fig.1-9).

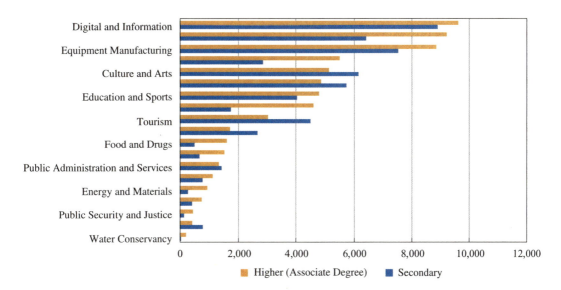

Fig. 1-8: Number of School Locations Offering Majors by Category in Secondary Vocational and Higher Vocational Education (Associate Degree) in 2024 [1]

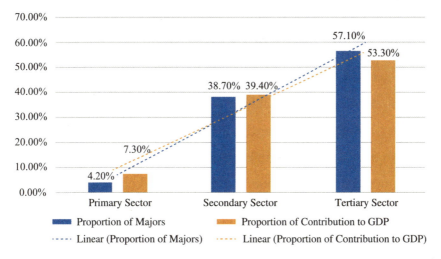

Fig. 1-9: Proportion of Majors and Corresponding Contribution of Sectors to GDP [2]

---

1   Catalog of Vocational Education Majors (2021) is classified based on the National Economic Industry Classification (GB/T 4754—2017).

2   Catalog of Vocational Education Majors (2021) is classified based on the National Economic Industry Classification (GB/T 4754—2017).

2. Creating a Dynamic Mechanism for Adjusting Majors

Sector-specific vocational education teaching advisory boards routinely publish the Guidance Report on Industry Talent Requirements and Vocational College Majors. The Ministry of Education and provincial education administrations jointly implement a mechanism for early warnings and dynamic adjustments of vocational education majors, gradually expanding the authority of vocational schools to establish distinctive programs independently. Since 2012, the average annual adjustment rate for higher vocational education majors has consistently exceeded 12%. In 2024, 6,068 new majors were introduced, and 5,052 were withdrawn, resulting in an adjustment rate of 17%.

3. Standardizing the Development of Talent Cultivating Programs

Vocational schools are required to develop their talent cultivating programs independently as per national teaching standards, taking into account regional development needs, educational characteristics, and professional realities. These programs should be designed to clearly outline professional training objectives and specify the essential knowledge and skills students need to acquire, continually enhancing their vocational adaptability and capabilities for sustainable development. Schools are mandated to standardize the establishment of general basic courses (including academic courses) and professional (skill-oriented) courses to strengthen students' professional competencies and work ethic. Practical teaching hours account for more than 50% of total class hours. Over 140,000 courses have been developed through school-enterprise cooperation and digital-intelligence integration. In addition to providing academic credentials, these courses also allow students to obtain professional qualifications, skill level certificates, and training certificates.

(III) Continuously Innovating Skilled Talent Cultivating Models

1. Consistently Implementing the Apprenticeship Training Model

Leveraging the modern apprenticeship model and the new enterprise apprenticeship model as pivotal strategies, China is actively enhancing its industry-education integration and promoting the dual-track system of school-enterprise collaboration in talent development. Since 2014, the Ministry of Education has launched national pilot projects rooted in the modern apprenticeship model in three phases, spanning over 1,000 majors and benefiting more than 100,000 students. Simultaneously, the Ministry of Human Resources and Social Security has encouraged the broad implementation of the new enterprise apprenticeship model in enterprise-school partnerships to improve on-the-job skills and facilitate training for career transitions, upgrading the competencies of employees within enterprises.

2. Exploring Classroom-based Teaching Reforms

Innovative teaching formats, such as "Industrial Park Classrooms," "Farm Classrooms," and "Workshop Classrooms," have been introduced to enhance students' vocational skills, professionalism, and work ethics within a production environment. The extensive implementation of scenario-based teaching, case studies, and project-based learning aligns with the skills training model for talent development. A variety of differentiated teaching methods, including collective instruction, group teaching, and personalized tutoring, are adaptively employed to meet the diverse abilities of students, helping them discover suitable learning modalities and development opportunities that align with their individual needs.

3. Empowering Skilled Talent Cultivating via Digital Technologies

As of now, 73.24% of vocational schools have been connected to provincial and municipal education networks, with 57.77% achieving comprehensive digital connectivity across their campuses. Since 2015, the Ministry of Education has established 1,152 experimental and pilot digital campuses among vocational schools, an initiative executed in five phases. Nearly 55% of vocational school teachers have embraced mixed teaching methodologies, utilizing hybrid virtual and physical environments, scenario simulations, human-machine collaboration, and a variety of other tools to facilitate smart learning. This approach has resulted in "panoramic classrooms" that integrate teaching content, course resources, and real-world workplace scenarios to enhance the overall learning experience.

(IV) Consistently Refining the Quality Evaluation System

A three-tiered evaluation system has been created, encompassing national, local, and school levels, to guide vocational schools in maintaining appropriate educational trajectories, ensuring their teaching quality, and enhancing the appeal of vocational education. At the national level, evaluation indicators have undergone consistent refinement. Since 2004, five rounds of assessments, supervision, and inspections of vocational schools have been conducted at the national level, gradually strengthening internal quality assurance systems and operational frameworks within vocational education. An annual reporting system for quality at the national, provincial, and school levels has been implemented to highlight vocational education's achievements and actively invite oversight from society. At the local level, innovative evaluation practices tailored to local characteristics have been developed. Notable examples include Shanghai's approach, which combines periodic self-assessments by schools with random municipal re-examinations, Hunan's random testing system for evaluating professional skill teaching capabilities at higher vocational colleges, and Liaoning's star-rated professional evaluation system. At the school level, a more sophisticated internal quality assurance system is gradually taking shape alongside mechanisms for teaching diagnosis and enhancement.

(V) Continuous Rise in Student and Social Satisfaction

1. Graduate Satisfaction Exceeding 92%

Surveys conducted in 2023, the satisfaction rate of vocational school graduates nationwide exceeded 92%, with a rate of 94.42% for secondary vocational graduates, 93.10% for junior college vocational graduates, and 92.70% for undergraduate vocational graduates. Additionally, 73.78% of higher vocational students are willing to recommend higher vocational schools to friends and family, with the recommendation rate for schools participating in the "Double High-Level Plan" reaching 81.68% (Fig. 1–10).

2. Parent Satisfaction Exceeding 95%

Surveys conducted in 2023 among parents of students from over 6,000

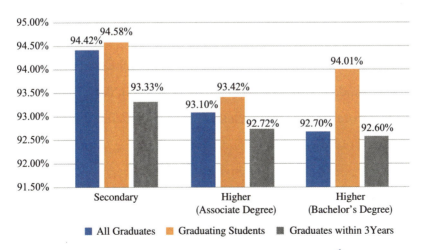

Fig. 1–10: Satisfaction Rate Among Graduates in 2023 [1]

---

1   Source: China Vocational Education Quality Annual Report and Data Collection Platform.

secondary and higher vocational schools nationwide indicated an overall satis-faction rate of 95.23%. Satisfaction rates among these parents were 95.42% for secondary vocational schools, 94.54% for associate degree higher vocational schools, and 95.19% for bachelor's degree vocational schools (Fig. 1–11).

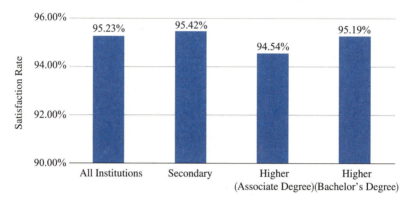

Fig. 1–11: Satisfaction Rate Among Parents of Vocational School Students in 2023 [1]

3. Employer Satisfaction with Graduates Exceeding 93%

Surveys conducted in 2023 among employers of graduates from more than 6,000 secondary and higher vocational schools revealed a satisfaction rate of 94.37% for secondary vocational school graduates, 95.94% for associate degree higher vocational school graduates, and 97.3% for bachelor's degree vocational school graduates, demonstrating an improvement from 2022. Employers highly commend the professionalism, specialized skills, and adaptability of vocational graduates (Fig. 1–12).

1   Source: China Vocational Education Quality Annual Report and Data Collection Platform.

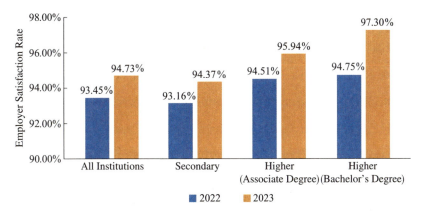

Fig. 1-12: Satisfaction Rate Among Employers of Vocational School Graduates in 2022 and 2023 [1]

IV. Providing Robust Support for Economic and Social Development

In recent years, China's vocational education has been playing an increasingly vital role in supporting regional and industrial development, supplying skilled talents for various industries, and raising the nation's overall intensity and capacity in promoting social equity and common prosperity.

(I) Developing a Structural Layout to Serve Regional Growth

1. Aligning the Layout of Educational Institutions with Provincial Development Needs

China has consistently emphasized the essential role of vocational education in promoting regional development. The country is actively involved in constructing, integrating, and adjusting secondary and higher vocational schools

---

1   Source: China Vocational Education Quality Annual Report and Data Collection Platform.

to enhance the distribution of vocational education within provinces. Currently, every provincial-level administrative unit in the nation operates vocational schools, with an average of 308 secondary vocational schools and 52 higher vocational schools per province. Among the 333 prefectural-level administrative divisions, 312 host higher vocational institutions, averaging five institutions per division. Many of these schools serve as the sole higher education establishments in their respective cities, serving a critical role in fostering sustainable economic and social development at the local level (Fig. 1–13).

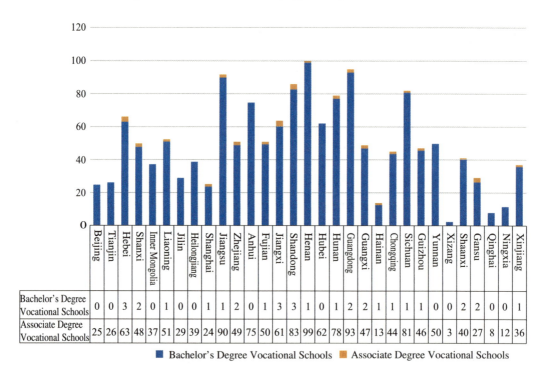

	Beijing	Tianjin	Hebei	Shanxi	Inner Mongolia	Liaoning	Jilin	Heilongjiang	Shanghai	Jiangsu	Zhejiang	Anhui	Fujian	Jiangxi	Shandong	Henan	Hubei	Hunan	Guangdong	Guangxi	Hainan	Chongqing	Sichuan	Guizhou	Yunnan	Xizang	Shaanxi	Gansu	Qinghai	Ningxia	Xinjiang
Bachelor's Degree Vocational Schools	0	0	3	2	0	1	0	0	1	1	2	0	1	3	3	1	0	1	2	2	1	1	1	1	0	0	2	2	0	0	1
Associate Degree Vocational Schools	25	26	63	48	37	51	29	39	24	90	49	75	50	61	83	99	62	78	93	47	13	44	81	46	50	3	40	27	8	12	36

■ Bachelor's Degree Vocational Schools   ■ Associate Degree Vocational Schools

Fig. 1–13: Number of Higher Vocational Schools by Province in 2022 [1]

2. Clusterizing Services to Support the Nation's Coordinated Interregional Development Strategies

In 2018, China initiated strategies to foster coordinated interregional de-

---

1   Source: National Education Development Statistical Bulletin (2022).

velopment, focusing on key areas such as the Beijing-Tianjin-Hebei region, the Yangtze River Delta, Guangdong-Hong Kong-Macao Greater Bay Area, and the Chengdu-Chongqing Economic Circle. Coordinating and matching vocational education resources has been a critical part of this initiative. Since 2018, several vocational education alliances have been established, including the Greater Bay Area Vocational Education and Training (VET) Alliance and the Greater Bay Area Teacher Development Alliance, as well as the Special Vocational Education Park in Guangdong-Hong Kong-Macau Greater Bay Area and the Beijing-Tianjin-Hebei Vocational Education Reform Demonstration Zone. These regional vocational education clusters have become platforms for central-local communication and interregional collaborations, propelling regional strategies to higher levels.

(II) Supplying Skilled Talents and Services Urgently Needed by Industries

1. Supporting the Structural Transformation and Upgrading of Chinese Industries

Vocational education in China is closely aligned with the requirements of emerging productive forces. It is imperative to optimize the setup of majors and innovate training models to lay a solid groundwork for developing new productive forces by equipping them with a high-quality labor supply. In 2023, higher vocational schools introduced 1,266 new school locations offering majors related to strategic emerging industries, including next-generation information technology, high-end equipment manufacturing, new materials, and biotechnology—representing an 8.24% increase from the previous year and producing over 1.05 million graduates (Fig. 1–14).

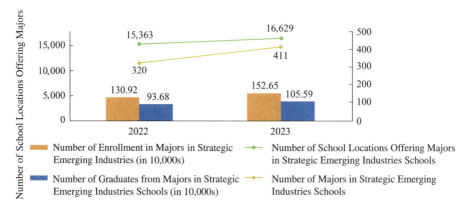

Fig 1–14: Layout of Majors in Higher Vocational Education Nationwide Aligning with Strategic Emerging Industries in 2022-2023 [1]

2. Collaborating with Chinese Enterprises to Address Front-Line Production Challenges

Rooted in the practical needs of regional industries, particularly small and medium-sized enterprises, vocational education in China actively works with businesses to deliver technical services, enhance processes, upgrade products, and facilitate the industrial application of technological advancements, assisting businesses in overcoming challenges faced at the frontline of production. In 2023, vocational schools concentrated on resolving technical and process-related issues in sectors such as new energy vehicles, intelligent manufacturing, and advanced materials. They undertook more than 2,700 national-level scientific research projects, reflecting a 7.52% increase compared to the previous year. Moreover, vocational schools provided technical services to companies through jointly established platforms, generating a cumulative value exceeding 9.1 billion yuan. Furthermore, these institutions transferred over 7,000 patent results, with the total value amounting to more than 540 million yuan (Fig. 1–15).

---

1   Source: China Vocational Education Quality Annual Report and Data Collection Platform.

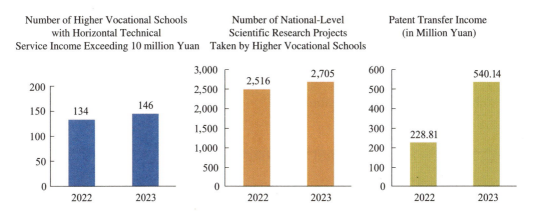

Fig 1-15: National Level Scientific Research Projects and Patent Transformation in Higher Vocational Schools in 2022-2023 [1]

(III) Highlighting Vocational Education's Role in Poverty Alleviation and Rural Revitalization

1. Providing Agricultural Training to Meet the Needs of Rural Revitalization

Vocational education programs are instrumental in providing local village officials and new agribusiness leaders with accessible educational opportunities close to home. These initiatives have successfully equipped rural communities with a substantial number of college-educated talents and professionals skilled in rural governance. The ongoing "Putonghua + Vocational Skills" training program specifically targets rural youth, preparing them for the workforce. Since 2013, the Ministry of Education, along with five other governmental bodies, has designated 261 counties nationwide as sites for vocational and adult education demonstration projects in rural settings, implemented in five phases. In 2019, the Ministry of Agriculture and Rural Affairs, in collaboration with the Ministry of Education, launched a strategic action plan to enhance the academic qualifications of one

---

1   Source: China Vocational Education Quality Annual Report and Data Collection Platform.

million farmers. To achieve the goal, over 100 institutions, recognized for their contributions to rural revitalization and agricultural research, jointly trained one million individuals, transforming them into leaders of rural revitalization efforts with higher education qualifications.

2. Advancing Agricultural Technology and Training Professional Agricultural Talents

Vocational schools train frontline agricultural workers in modern production techniques, promoting the adoption of new breeds, technologies, methods, and equipment. Across the nation, 274 agricultural vocational schools offer 35 distinct agricultural majors. Higher vocational schools boast nearly 700 majors, annually enrolling over 40,000 students and securing more than 600 intellectual property rights related to agriculture. In 2024, the Ministry of Agriculture and Rural Affairs designated the first group of 534 outstanding national field schools for rural farmers at the county level.

3. Implementing Targeted Support Between Eastern and Western Regions

To address regional development imbalances, a targeted support strategy was initiated by the Ministry of Education in 2001, encompassing three primary actions: "Comprehensive Vocational School Collaboration Across East and West," "Secondary Vocational Enrollment Guarantee in Eastern and Western Regions," and "Full Participation of Vocational Schools in East-West Labor Cooperation." A total investment exceeding 1.8 billion yuan (including equipment) has supported the creation of 683 majors, 338 training bases, and 63 branch campuses (teaching sites). Additionally, the initiative has provided employment skills training for over 140,000 individuals and job skill enhancement training for more than 160,000 individuals. These efforts have significantly expanded the pool of skilled professionals needed for the high-quality development of the Western regions.

(IV) Raising the Employment Quality and Rate

1. Maintaining High Placement Rates for Graduates

The Chinese government strongly emphasizes youth employment, offering graduates an array of career services and pathways through special employment services. From 2022 to 2024, placement rates for graduates from secondary vocational schools remained robust, at 94.70%, 94.44%, and 93.96%, respectively. Graduates from higher vocational institutions also demonstrated strong outcomes with placement rates of 90.60%, 91.88%, and 93.55%, respectively, maintaining high overall level (Fig. 1–16).

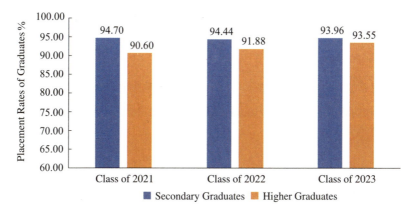

Fig 1–16: Employment Placement Rates of Graduates of Secondary Vocational Schools and Higher Vocational Schools from 2021 to 2023 [1]

2. Consistently Improving Employment Quality of Graduates

The Chinese government adheres to an employment-first policy, concentrating on securing high-quality employment for graduates. Through ongoing targeted initiatives such as "Party Secretaries and Principals of Higher Vocational Schools Visiting Enterprises for More Job Opportunities" "10,000 Enterprises

---

1   Source: China Vocational Education Quality Annual Report and Data Collection Platform.

on Campus," and "24365 Campus Online Recruitment," the government has bolstered graduates' entry into quality employment. In the past three years, the alignment between graduates' fields of study from higher vocational schools and their job placements has consistently improved. For the class of 2023, the match rate reached 72.17%, an increase of 4.75% from 2021 (Fig. 1–17). Moreover, the average starting salary for these graduates rose to 4,082.20 yuan, marking an 11.13% increase since 2021 (Fig. 1–18).

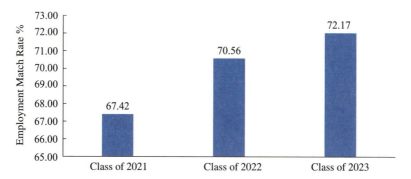

Fig. 1–17: Employment Match Rates of Graduates from Higher Vocational Schools from 2021 to 2023 [1]

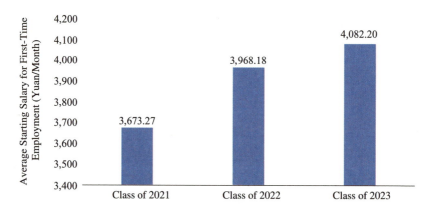

Fig. 1–18: Average Starting Salary for First-Time Employment of Graduates from Higher Vocational Schools from 2021 to 2023 [2]

---

1   Source: China Vocational Education Quality Annual Report and Data Collection Platform.
2   Source: China Vocational Education Quality Annual Report and Data Collection Platform.

3. Assisting Veterans in Securing High-Quality Employment

In recent years, the Ministry of Education and the Ministry of Veterans Affairs have worked together to enhance academic education for veterans, enabling 1.073 million veterans to enroll in higher vocational education. Additionally, 95,000 veterans have been supported in advancing to undergraduate studies through vocational adaptability assessments or comprehensive vocational skills evaluations. Partnerships between educational institutions and businesses, along with inter-provincial and cross-regional training programs, have collectively benefited over one million veterans.

4. Expanding Talent Development in Eldercare and Childcare

In response to the nation's demographic shifts, Chinese vocational education has been broadening the scope and scale of majors in eldercare and childcare. Since 2021, the annual growth rate in establishing majors for people's livelihood such as Intelligent Health Management for the Elderly, Modern Home Management and Services, and Infant and Toddler Care Management at higher vocational schools has exceeded 5%. By 2024, there have been 3,480 registered majors eldercare and childcare, with a total of 415,000 graduates from higher vocational schools..

V. Becoming a New Force in International Educational Exchanges and Cooperation

Adhering to the development principles of innovation, coordination, environmental consciousness, openness, and sharing, the Chinese government strategically oversees vocational education bringing in and going global. This encompasses building platforms for international exchanges and cooperation, fostering a consensus on vocational education development, sharing China's vocational education solutions, and collaborating with nations worldwide to advance vocational education. China's vocational education outreach predominantly focuses on development collaborations with countries involved in the Belt and Road Initiative, particularly in Asia and Africa, emphasizing sectors such as energy and chemical engineering, logistics management, and equipment manufacturing. The programs are often co-run by Chinese institutions or globalized Chinese corporations in partnership with foreign governments, businesses, or educational institutions.

(I) Getting Actively Involved in Global Vocational Education Cooperation

1. Researching Digital and Green Development of Vocational Education in Partnership Within UNESCO Network

Utilizing the network of CVED and other five centers of UNESCO International Centers for Technical and Vocational Education and Training (UNEVOC Center), and a UNESCO Chair on Digitalization in TVET at Shenzhen Polytechnic University, researches on the digitalization of vocational education, the development of green skills, international cooperation and other topics are conducted with UNESCO bodies and member entities..

2. Enhancing Life Skills of Vocational Students in Partnership with UNICEF

CVED leads a youth development project aimed at bolstering the "life skills" (core competencies in Chinese) of students at vocational schools. This project aims to enhance students' self-awareness, problem-solving skills, interpersonal relations, emotional management, critical and creative thinking, as well as green and digital skills, thereby equipping them to thrive in future social and economic settings. Now in its third five-year cycle, the project has expanded to include 134 vocational schools across 19 provinces, bringing vocational students to join events by the United Nations in China, such as "A Green Future, Her Power" Asia-Pacific Summit and "Green Skills" Youth Consultation Dialogues.

3. Enhancing the Quality Development of Vocational Skills Competitions in Partnership with WorldSkills

China has consistently participated in the WorldSkills Competition, securing 57 gold, 32 silver, and 24 bronze medals over the years, ranking first on the gold medal tally in the 2017, 2019, 2022, and 2024 competitions. These achievements highlight the exceptional pursuit of excellence and proactive ethos among Chinese youth. In collaboration with WorldSkills, China is actively preparing to host the 48th WorldSkills Competition.

(II) Building an International Exchange and Cooperation Platform

China has actively integrated high-quality vocational education resources both from home and abroad by forming international alliances, hosting global forums, and engaging in a variety of cooperative projects. Key regional cooperation mechanisms have been established, such as the Belt and Road Vocational Education Alliance, the Future of Africa—Vocational Education Cooperation Plan, the BRICS Technical and Vocational Education and Training (TVET) Cooperation Alliance, the China-Central and Eastern European Countries Vocational School Industry-Education Alliance, the China-ASEAN Vocational Education Federation, the Silk Road Eurasian Vocational Education Institutions Alliance, the New Land-Sea Corridor Vocational Education International Cooperation Alliance, and the Lancang-Mekong Vocational Education Alliance. Furthermore, China has initiated the World Vocational and Technical Education Development

Conference, which has become a distinguished international vocational education public service brand, incorporating conferences, alliances, awards, competitions, and exhibitions.

 Column

President Xi Jinping's Congratulatory Letter to the 2022 World Vocational and Technical Education Development Conference

Vocational education is closely linked with economic and social development, and has great significance for promoting employment and entrepreneurship, boosting economic and social development, and improving people's well-being. China actively pushes for ward the high-quality development of vocational education, and supports exchanges and cooperation in vocational education with other countries. The Chinese side stands ready to work with other countries in the world to strengthen mutual learning, joint contribution, and shared benefits, join hands to implement the Global Development Initiative, and contribute to accelerating the implementation of the United Nations 2030 Agenda for Sustainable Development.

(III) Sharing of Chinese Solutions Proactively

While vigorously developing its vocational education system, China actively learns from progressive practices worldwide and reciprocates by sharing its own experience with the rest of the world.

1. Co-Developing International Vocational Education Projects

Around 300 vocational schools from 27 provinces, autonomous regions and municipalities directly under the central government have established approximately 400 institutions and programs in partnership with over 70 countries and regions, giving birth to a series of internationally recognized educational brands such as Luban Workshop, Chinese Language Workshop, Luban-Mozi College, Modern Craftsman Institute, Silk Road School (Table 1–3).

Table 1–3: Overview of Some Local International Vocational Education Brands

No.	Brand Name	Initiating Province	Year Established	Number of Partner Countries	Number of Establishments
1	Silk Road School	Zhejiang	2016	34	52
2	Zheng He Academy	Jiangsu	2018	9	9
3	Maritime Silk Road Schools	Fujian	2019	17	20
4	Luban-Mozi College	Shandong	2023	17	34
5	Mozi Institute	Liaoning	2023	14	16
6	China-ASEAN Modern Craftsman Institute	Guangxi	2023	10	17

2. Co-Founding Vocational Schools

Expanding upon existing project collaborations, China's vocational education sector has explored the creation of vocational schools with countries and regions participating in the Belt and Road Initiative, to cultivate high-quality skilled professionals for local markets. For example, Nanjing Vocational University of Industry Technology, in collaboration with the Federation of Khmer Chinese in Cambodia, founded the Cambodia-China University of Technology and Science (CamTech). The university now offers seven majors and has trained over 3,000 students for the local market through school-enterprise cooperative order-oriented classes. Similarly, Tianjin University of Technology and Education and Ethiopia have collaboratively established the Federal Technical and Vocational Training Institute (FTVTI), which offers 22 undergraduate programs and has produced over 5,000 graduates.

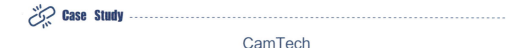 **Case Study** ---

CamTech

On December 20, 2023, CamTech was officially established through a partnership between Nanjing Vocational University of Industry Technology and the Federation of Khmer Chinese in Cambodia. This university is focused on nurturing local technical talent, aiming to provide vocational undergraduate education through various study models like 4+0, 2+2, and 3+1. Students have the opportunity to earn degrees and diplomas from both China and Cambodia after completing four years of study. Currently, CamTech offers seven undergraduate programs: New Energy Power Engineering Technology, Automotive Service Engineering Technology, Network Engineering Technology, E-commerce, Modern Logistics Management, Tourism Management, and Mechanical and Electronic Engineering Technology. CamTech not only upgrades the reach of China's shared vocational education solutions but also marks an innovative and experimental step in creating a regional vocational education community.

3. Training a Large Number of Skilled Talents for Partner Countries

To date, more than 30 Luban Workshops in Asia, Europe and Africa have collectively provided vocational education for over 10,000 students, and training for more than 31,000 participants (person-time). In collaboration with ten Chinese vocational schools, the Chinese non-ferrous metal industry founded the Sino-Zam Vocational College of Science and Technology. Nearly 90% of its first graduating class in 2023 secured employment with local Chinese-funded companies. Moreover, by establishing the China-Laos cooperation pilot station, Guangxi Vocational University of Agriculture has trained nearly 2,000 local agricultural technicians and over 10,000 farmers (person-time), introducing 67 high-quality crop breeds across more than 6,589 acres. This initiative received the outstanding contribution award from the Ministry of Agriculture and Forestry of Laos and stands as a paragon of China-Laos cooperation.

4. Consistently Increasing International Influence

Chinese vocational education institutions have steadily gained recognition in host countries through genuine cooperation and the provision of high-quality educational resources. Leaders from Uzbekistan, Laos, Vietnam, and Sri Lanka, among others, have openly praised the excellence of China's vocational education when meeting with Chinese leaders, expressing eagerness to learn from China's successful experience in vocational education. At the 2022 World Vocational and Technical Education Development Conference, the Ethiopian Minister of Labour and Skills, Muferihat Kamil Ahmed, called for an expansion of Luban Workshop across Ethiopia in her keynote speech. During Kenyan President Ruto's visit to China for the Third Belt and Road Forum for International Cooperation, he expressed his gratitude to China for its support to Kenya on human resource training among others since 2014, which has benefited 140 institutions and increased the number of trained individuals from 90,000 to 350,000, equipping the country with essential skills for economic and social development.

Chapter Two: Valuable Experience

Vocational education in China has significantly evolved in parallel with the country's economic development and consistently benefitted from mutual exchanges with international peers. In 2012, over four decades after the Reform and Opening-up, these initiatives have helped China develop unique strengths in vocational education while obtaining a wealth of valuable experience.

I. Maximizing the Government's Role in Coordination and Promotion

China places strategic emphasis on the development of vocational education, treating it as a critical public service. The Chinese government consistently enhances institutional innovation, policy support, and financial support to bolster this vital sector.

1. Governing Vocational Education on Legal Basis and Building a Robust Legal Framework

The amended *Vocational Education Law of the People's Republic of China (2022),* hereinafter referred to as the *Vocational Education Law*, provides a legal basis for vocational education as a distinct educational category. It specifies the responsibilities of governments at all levels and various types of vocational schools, and the roles of industries and businesses in delivering vocational education. Since the enactment of the *Vocational Education Law*, different provinces have introduced their local vocational education regulations and specific legal laws. For example, Shandong Province's *Vocational Education Regulations* promote collaboration among businesses, schools, and research institutions in talent development, scientific research, and technological services. Similarly, Tianjin introduced the *Regulations on the Promotion of Industry-Education Integration in Vocational Education* to support the formation of regional industry-education integration communities and industry chain industry-education integration communities, advancing their operational implementation. Guided by the *Vocational Education Law*, the vocational education legal and regulatory system, comprised of relevant national and local laws and regulations, departmental rules, and normative documents, continues to be refined, ensuring that vocational education develops steadily along the path of legal governance.

2. Enhancing High-Level Coordination and System Supply

By regularly holding national conferences on vocational education, establishing inter-departmental joint meeting systems at various levels, and creating mechanisms for soliciting public opinions on major decisions, China is able to unify thoughts, build consensus, and make a collective force to guide the direction of vocational education reform and invigorate vocational education. Since 2012, at the national level, two vocational education conferences have been convened, the State Council has issued four vocational education-specific reform documents, and the Ministry of Education has released 27 vocational education reform documents. These reform measures cover multiple areas, including top-level design of vocational education, diversified governance, talent development, policy incentives, and institutional guarantees, specifying reform directions and development strategies at critical junctures in the development of vocational education, thus forming the major framework of China's vocational education reform and development.

3. Strengthening Central-Local Communication and Innovating Joint Development Mechanisms for Reforms

The central government supports local initiatives that adapt reforms to regional conditions by selecting provinces and municipal governments from the eastern, central, and western parts of China with the foundations and will to advance critical reforms. Since 2019, the State Council has incentivized approximately five provinces annually that have demonstrated significant progress in vocational education reforms for four consecutive years. Since 2020, the Ministry of Education has worked with eleven provinces including Shandong, Gansu, and Jiangxi to establish vocational education innovation and development highlands, creating a reform framework that integrates all administrative levels and facilitates interregional coordination. This framework deepens vocational education reforms across entire provinces and urban clusters. In 2023, comprehensive trials to advance the modern vocational education system reform were initiated in eight provinces, further innovating mechanisms for central-local communication, interregional collaboration, and multi-party coordination. These mechanisms have significantly boosted local enthusiasm for developing and innovating vocational education, promoting education that serves regional development strategies and achieving differentiated growth with local characteristics.

4. Ramping Up Investment and Supporting Broad and Equitable Participation by Social Forces

Emphasizing vocational education's nature as a public benefit, public institutions remain at the forefront of ensuring that vocational education is accessible to all. Since 2012, public funding for vocational education has seen consistent growth: investment in higher vocational education increased from 141 billion yuan in 2012 to 202.3 billion yuan in 2017 and 363 billion yuan in 2023, and secondary vocational education funding rose from 231.9 billion yuan in 2017 to 330.9 billion yuan in 2023. In the meantime, the Chinese government also attaches great importance to coordinating educational resources, employing a variety of support mechanisms, such as government subsidies, funds, and donation incentives, to encourage social investment in vocational schools. By 2023, social forces have established 2,128 secondary vocational schools, representing 25% of the total, and 396 higher vocational schools, accounting for 30%.

II. Highlighting the Coordinated Development of Vocational Education with Economic and Social Progress

Vocational education has been integrated into China's overall plans for national economic and social development. It is based on the industrial layout and business development needs within regions, with adjustments made dynamically to the setting of majors and talent training standards, enabling industries and businesses to collaborate with vocational schools in talent training, technological research and development, and social services.

1. Creating a National Mechanism for the Release and Matching of Industrial Talent Supply and Demand

National vocational education teaching advisory boards of industries routinely organize research and publish guidance reports on talent demand and major setting, while the Ministry of Human Resources and Social Security releases information on the supply and demand of skilled talent in various industries. Responding to the skilled talent structure needed by the modern industrial system, based on the National Economic Industry Classification, the Vocational Classification Canon, and the New Occupations Catalog, the Ministry of Education compiles and periodically revises the catalog of vocational education majors, grounded in a science-based analysis of industry, occupations, positions, and the interrelations of majors.

2. Enabling Local Governments and Vocational Schools to Respond to Regional Economic Developments Promptly

Local educational administrative departments have been aligning local vocational education with regional industrial development plans and guiding vocational schools to match their resources and major setting with the regional industrial structure through measures such as major registrations, performance evaluations, and funding allocations. By establishing major-building advisory boards and incorporating businesses in talent training, vocational schools regularly visit businesses to expand job opportunities and understand business needs, enabling them to respond more promptly to employers' demands. For example, during the "14th Five-Year Plan", Anhui Province focused on developing emerging industries, including new energy vehicles, artificial intelligence, advanced photovoltaics, and new energy storage. To achieve this goal, the Anhui Provincial Department of Education took the initiative to introduce ten measures, including study-employment alignment and early warning mechanisms, providing incentives for programs serving emerging and future industries. Currently, vocational education majors serving these ten emerging industries in Anhui account for 58.12% of the total, enhancing the capability of skilled talent to support industrial innovation and development.

3. Encouraging Vocational Schools to Support Businesses in Technological Improvements and Upgrades

Support is given to vocational schools to enhance their role in assisting regional businesses to transform and upgrade, make technological improvements, upgrade products, optimize processes, and promote applications. These supportive efforts include introducing high-level faculty and business technicians and increasing the weight of industrial development innovation in teacher performance evaluations. For example, Hangzhou Vocational & Technical College joined hands with XIO Lift company to tackle technical challenges such as the construction of ultra-long escalators and smart elevator monitoring platforms. This partnership not only boosted the company's competitive edge in the market but also helped the college gain recognition within the industry for its talent cultivation and technical services, with the employment rate for graduates in relevant majors hitting an impressive 98.59%.

III. Focusing on Innovation in Models for Talent Development of Industry-Education Integration and Work-Integrated Learning

China's vocational education consistently upholds the principles of industry-education integration and school-enterprise collaboration, highlighting work-integrated learning and the unity of knowing and doing. China focuses on building an educational ecosystem where schools and enterprises jointly nurture future talents and a sophisticated institutionalized mechanism connecting schools and enterprises, enabling students to develop practical skills and adaptability in real-world production environments.

1. Promoting Industry-Education Integration Through Sector-Specific Industry-Education Integration Communities and Municipal Industry-Education Consortium

Sector-specific industry-education integration communities emphasize the role of central and local leading enterprises and key industry players in leading cross-regional initiatives, centralizing high-quality industry resources to enhance the quality of talent development across industries. Large state-owned enterprises such as CRRC and Aluminum Corporation of China Limited have taken active steps by integrating school-enterprise co-developed technology, talents, resources, and culture. They have established platforms, mechanisms, and strong measures, creating a new industry-education integration pattern where schools and enterprises are unified, education and industry are fully integrated, training and education are organically combined, and both parties jointly provide education. This model has set a perfect example for leading enterprises to get involved in providing high-quality vocational education. Municipal industry-education consortium leverages the coordinating role of industrial park governments to foster cooperation in technological innovation and talent development between resident enterprises and relevant educational institutions, thus enhancing vocational schools' ability to serve local economic development with higher precision. For example, the Jinjiang Municipal Industry-Education Consortium based in Jinjiang Economic Development Zone is the only county-level organization of its kind in China. With a current enrollment of 58,000 students, it has trained 19,000 full-time graduates in 2023, provided community training to 56,000 participants, facilitated 1,289 industry-education-research cooperation projects with investments exceeding 1 billion yuan, and provided multi-level, full-cycle skilled talent support and technical services to various enterprises in Jinjiang.

2. Enhancing School-Enterprise Collaboration Through Industry-Education Integrated Cities and Enterprises

China has established the "finance + fiscal + land + credit" incentive mechanism to attract significant industrial cities and leading enterprises to support and participate in vocational education. The National Development and Reform Commission has recognized 21 national pilot cities for industry-education integration, and the Ministry of Education has identified 299 exemplary vocational education groups (alliances). Over 4,600 industry-education integrated enterprises nationwide, as well as a large number of industry organizations and associations, are actively participating in industry-education integration efforts. These initiatives have created the preliminary promotion mechanism for school-enterprise collaboration, with cities as connections, industries as key support points, and enterprises as the main focus.

3. Implementing a Full-Process Transition Mechanism to Achieve Work-Integrated Learning and the Unity of Knowing and Doing

Vocational schools typically work closely with enterprises to co-enroll, co-train, and co-assess students, utilizing a career-based success strategy to achieve a seamless transition from campus learning to employment. In this model, learners can be students in schools and employees in companies at the same time. They can enjoy student support policies in schools, as well as work opportunities and work allowances offered by companies. At the same time, schools and enterprises co-develop talent training programs, curricula, and textbooks that match the actual tasks required for roles in enterprises. Teachers and technicians from both schools and enterprises form a joint mentoring team to share teaching responsibilities and plan students' learning and practical experiences both in classrooms and on the job. This approach effectively enhances the relevance and applicability of school training, tackling issues like low job suitability and high post-employment training costs for companies.

IV. Positioning Quality Construction as the Core in Promoting Development

Chinese vocational education steadfastly adheres to the principle of fostering virtue through education, as well as the simultaneous cultivation of morality and skills. Propelled by teaching reforms, the construction of "Double-Qualified" teacher teams, and digital transformation, China aims to enhance the quality of talent development at vocational schools.

1. Positioning "Fostering Virtue Through Education" as the Fundamental Evaluation Standard for the Quality of Vocational Schools

China consistently prioritizes the comprehensive development of individuals as the primary goal of vocational education. By strengthening standard-led guidance and government oversight, and through the establishment of unified national standards for general basic courses, China provides high-quality liberal arts education to students, ensuring educational institutions serve their fundamental function of nurturing talents. Various vocational schools prioritize skill training and moral education equally, considering the socialist core values practiced by students as a critical component of their comprehensive quality assessment. Schools, industries, and enterprises work closely to enhance the vocational school teacher cultivation and training mechanisms, improve mental health service systems for students, and establish a system of scholarships and financial aids, all of which support the holistic development of students in moral, intellectual, physical, artistic, and labor education.

2. Focusing on Standards and Projects to Drive Quality Improvement

China has developed a sophisticated system of vocational education standards that plays a crucial and guiding role in standardizing talent cultivation, enhancing industry-education integration, and ensuring quality development. Vocational schools are encouraged to develop distinctive characteristics based on these standards. National projects facilitate cross-departmental collaboration, leverage local investments, stimulate motivation, and strengthen guidance. Recent national-level initiatives, such as the construction of high-level vocational colleges and clusters of majors, national online excellent courses, teaching resource databases for vocational majors, vocational school teacher quality improvement programs, national vocational education teacher innovation teams, and teaching skills competitions, have effectively enhanced the key school-running capacities and self-directed development of vocational schools.

3. Enhancing the Quality of Vocational Education via Digital Empowerment

The core objective of digitalization in vocational education is to improve the quality and efficiency of education and to cultivate high-quality skilled talents adapted to the digital age. In the process of digitalization, China maintains a systemic perspective, emphasizing system integration with long-term strategic planning as well as phased, step-by-step implementation. In 2022, the approach of "Connection, Content, Cooperation" (3C) was adopted, gradually moving towards "Integrated, Intelligent, International" (3I), steadily advancing the in-depth development of digital vocational education. In the meantime, advanced technologies such as cloud computing, big data, and artificial intelligence are actively employed to promote the digital upgrading of teaching content, methods, and tools, enhancing students' learning experiences and outcomes. Smart Education of China, launched in 2022, won the UNESCO Prize for ICT in education, representing a core achievement of China's strategy for the digitalization of vocational education.

4. Establishing a Normalized Quality Improvement Mechanism via Competitions and Evaluations

High-quality national competitions promote the implementation of national standards in talent training, motivating vocational schools to reform and innovation momentum. In recent years, major vocational education events and awards, such as the National Vocational College Skills Competition, National Teaching Achievement Awards, and National Textbook Construction Awards, have introduced a series of original and pioneering teaching reform achievements. The creation of regular on-campus cyclical mechanisms for teaching diagnosis and improvement encourages Chinese vocational schools to carry out diagnostic and enhancement at multiple levels and from various angles based on their educational philosophy, positioning, and talent training goals. This approach continuously strengthens their internal teaching quality assurance system.

V. Deepening International Exchange and Cooperation Through Mutual Learning and Shared Benefits

1. Building a Platform for Mutual Learning in Vocational Education

Over the past four decades since the Reform and Opening-up, the Chinese government, Chinese educational institutions, and Chinese social organizations have established cooperative relationships with countries such as Germany, the United Kingdom, and Australia. These partnerships focus on actively learning from nations excelling in vocational education—particularly their latest research and practical outcomes in areas like talent cultivating patterns, curriculum development models, pedagogical reforms, and school-enterprise collaboration mechanisms. By integrating experiences from these countries with Chinese practices, China has gradually developed its own theoretical research achievements and operational experiences. On this foundation, China has created a global vocational education platform that incorporates conferences, alliances, awards, competitions, and exhibitions, inviting vocational education peers from around the world to share development experiences and discuss future paths.

2. Sharing Development Achievements in Vocational Education

Through platforms and cooperatives like the World Federation for Vocational and Technical Education Development and the World Vocational and Technical Education Development Conference (WVTEDC), China is actively involved in the global governance of vocational education. China combines its vocational education efforts with international collaborations in industrial capacity, poverty reduction, and emissions reduction. It employs an approach that integrates academic education with vocational training, sharing China's vocational education methodologies, technologies, and standards with the rest of the world. By founding training centers, supplying advanced teaching equipment, and deploying Chinese educators and technicians to develop skilled talent in partner countries, China has created successful vocational education brands such as Luban Workshop and Center for Chinese Language and Professional Skills. These initiatives position China as a major global provider of public vocational education resources.

Chapter Three: Strategic Tasks

China has currently entered a new phase of further comprehensive deepening reforms and advancing Chinese-style modernization, establishing the ambitious goal of becoming a leading education power by 2035. China is committed to building a vocational education system that empowers the integration of vocational education and general education, as well as industry-education integration. This effort aims to further promote the integration of vocational education with industries, local and government policies, regional and social structures, and individual lifelong learning. The ultimate goal is to cultivate a greater number of highly skilled talents, outstanding artisans and Craftsmen of the Nation.

I. Enhancing the Capacity of Vocational Education to Serve National Development Strategies

Developing new productive forces relies heavily on high-quality labor. Vocational education must be deeply rooted in regions and integrated with industries to accelerate the training of talent needed to upgrade traditional industries, expand emerging industries, and grow future industries.

1. Reinforcing Vocational Education's Connection to Regional Economies

Serving the development of regional economies and societies is a crucial task for vocational education. Educational institutions should actively align their educational positioning, services, major structures, and social contributions with the needs of their local communities, thereby strengthening their connections to regional economic and social development. They should focus on growth through their services and seek support that reflects their contributions. Their primary goal should not be maximizing scale but rather optimizing their quality and alignment with genuine social needs. According to the industrial structures, resource endowments, and development stages of their regions, educational institutions should actively integrate into national key functional areas such as the Beijing-Tianjin-Hebei region, the Yangtze River Delta, Guangdong-Hong Kong-Macao Greater Bay Area, and the Chengdu-Chongqing Economic Circle to better serve the economic and social development of provinces and cities.

2. Reinforcing Vocational Education's Compatibility with Industrial Needs

China has a comprehensive and large-scale industrial system with a sophisticated and resilient industrial chain. The vocational education sector should closely align with all segments of the industrial chain, focusing on key industrial clusters such as advanced manufacturing and digital industries, along with essential industries and fields. The sector should also enhance skills training for critical positions in manufacturing, assembly, operation, and maintenance; promote the sharing of resources between industry and education; encourage effective school-enterprise collaboration in talent training and technological innovation; and promptly adapt the offerings of majors and talent training structures based on the evolving needs of industries to ensure an effective supply of skilled workforce.

3. Reinforcing the School-Running Capacities and Service Quality of Vocational Schools

Vocational schools should strive to achieve excellent school-running capacities and high-quality industry-education integration as their developmental directions, shifting from focusing solely on improving educational conditions and self-sustaining development to a broader focus on serving industrial and societal development, with an emphasis on serving national strategies, integrating into regional development, and promoting industrial upgrades. Vocational schools need to deepen reform, enhance their school-running capacities, and dynamically optimize majors, curricula, textbooks, faculty, and practical training bases in response to technological advancements, industrial upgrades, and societal changes, shifting from merely imparting knowledge and providing traditional skills training to enhancing comprehensive and digital skills.

II. Expanding Channels for Student Growth and Success via the Integration of Vocational Education and General Education

China's changing demographics and growing access to higher education have opened up a variety of educational pathways and options. Educational institutions must adhere to the principle of "vocational education for all." This means ensuring that education is equitable and inclusive, catering to individual needs. Institutions should provide accessible, balanced, high-quality, and lifelong services that support learners' holistic and sustainable development.

1. Focusing on Vocational Education Enlightenment

Further progress should be made in integrating vocational education with general education, enabling elementary and secondary students to develop an understanding of labor and professional awareness through hands-on labor and professional experiences. This approach will help spark their interest and appreciation for professional skills and potential career paths early on. By planting these "seeds" now, we can set the foundation for their future career development and life planning, ultimately preparing them for successful professional journeys ahead.

2. Meeting the Diverse Development Needs of Students

The diversity of post-junior high education reflects the maturity, flexibility, and inclusiveness of the education system. Multiple pathways and training forms connecting vocational and general education should be created to provide students with opportunities and platforms for making various choices and receiving diversified talent training. Integration models between senior high school and undergraduate stages should also be enhanced to prepare students for the diverse challenges of future society.

3. Promoting Student Development Through Evaluation Reform

Continuous efforts are needed to ensure open channels for the growth of skilled talents. It's essential to refine and promote the "Cultural Literacy + Vocational Skills" dual-evaluation system in the Entrance Examination for Vocational College, to ensure that skilled talent training is heading in the right direction. Moreover, we should give more weight to evaluations by industrial enterprises and experiment with a comprehensive evaluation system that effectively assesses students' overall qualities and professional skills. By reforming evaluations, we can also enhance society's recognition of the quality of skilled talent training.

III. Facilitating Common Prosperity Through Vocational Education

Vocational education plays a vital role in building social human capital and improving people's well-being. It continues to contribute significantly to job creation, increasing the middle-income demographic, driving comprehensive rural revitalization, promoting common prosperity in both urban and rural settings, and enhancing the spiritual and cultural lives of the communities.

1. Enhancing the Fundamental Role of Vocational Education in Job Creation

Employment is the most important component of people's livelihoods. Vocational education and training is one of the most direct means to create job opportunities. It is crucial to coordinate vocational education, training, and employment policies, supporting various learners — including vocational school students, freelancers, migrant workers, and veterans — to further enhance their overall quality and employability through receiving vocational education and training. This support also enhances the capabilities of those who are currently employed. By doing this, we can address structural employment issues and assist more workers in moving into the middle-income group through their hard work.

2. Enhancing the Capability to Serve the Integrated Development of Urban and Rural Areas

Rural revitalization is a necessary path to achieving common prosperity, and the integrated development of urban and rural areas is an inevitable requirement of Chinese-style modernization. The approach to integrated development in urban and rural vocational education needs further innovation to optimize resource allocation and support the advancement of new urbanization. Moreover, vocational education should broaden its focus to include industrial workers, owners of small and medium-sized enterprises, self-employed individuals, new-type farmers, and vulnerable groups, such as students from low-income families in both rural and urban areas. This expansion aims to enhance professional development and decent employment opportunities for urban and rural workers.

3. Expanding Lifelong Learning Opportunities

Achieving common prosperity of material and spiritual life is a significant characteristic of the Chinese-style modernization. Vocational education should be more inclusive, actively meeting diverse cultural and spiritual needs of people across different ages and social classes. Leveraging the strengths of vocational schools in providing community-based education and setup of majors across all sectors of the national economy, we need to expedite the development of digital education infrastructure, create interconnected digital platforms and broaden access to high-quality digital resources of vocational education in both urban and rural areas. Additionally, we should enhance the curriculum service system to better support personalized and lifelong learning, ultimately empowering the establishment of a learning society.

IV. Fostering a Favorable Ecosystem for the Development of Vocational Education

Vocational education must proactively align with economic and social development while also garnering support from all sectors of society. Together, we will foster an ecosystem where everyone has the opportunity to succeed and to fully realize their potential through shared concepts, mechanisms, and environment.

1. Shaping a Correct Concept of Talent Cultivation Across Society

Revering labor and respecting workers are enduring virtues of the Chinese nation. We must continue to uphold the principles of simultaneous cultivation of morality and skills and the unity of knowing and doing. By consistently organizing events like Vocational Education Week and the "Model Workers and Craftsmen Entering Campuses," we can further promote the fashion of the times that glorifies labor, values skills and honors creativity, motivating more young people to develop their skills and dedicate those skills to the service of the country.

2. Establishing a New Collaborative Framework Among Government, Industries, Enterprises, and Educational Institutions

School-enterprise collaboration is a fundamental model for vocational education. We should further develop a collaborative framework for central-local communication, interregional collaboration, and multi-party coordination in vocational education development. At both national and provincial levels, the "finance + public economy + land + credit" incentives should be refined to better motivate and recognize enterprises as key contributors to the development of vocational education. By pooling resources such as funding, technology, talent, and policies, we can enhance the involvement of government, industry, enterprises, families, and social entities in vocational education.

3. Ensuring Smooth Career Development Channels for Skilled Talents

Skilled talents are an essential component of the national strategic talent pool. We must adopt more proactive, open, and effective talent policies to ensure that vocational school graduates enjoy the same rights as their counterparts from general education in terms of residency, employment, recruitment, professional title evaluation, and promotion. We should promote the new eight-tier worker system focused on skill levels and creative contributions, increasing the income of workers in the front line of production and service. Additionally, we need to enhance the recognition and rewards for highly skilled workers to foster enthusiasm, initiative, and creativity in their professional endeavors and entrepreneurial ventures.

V. Contributing to the Construction of a Community with a Shared Future for Humanity

Vocational education is closely linked to economic and social development and is pivotal to industrial advancement and the improvement of people's livelihoods. China's successful experiences in vocational education serve as a source of inspiration for the world to promote joint development through higher levels of openness.

1. Actively Getting Involved in the Global Governance of Vocational Education

China continues to deepen multilateral cooperation in the field of education and actively responds to the concepts and initiatives regarding global vocational education development proposed by international organizations such as UNESCO. Relying on regional and intergovernmental cooperation mechanisms and platforms for exchange and cooperation, China offers technical support and practical experiences in vocational education to a broad group of developing countries, sharing its achievements in the digital transformation of vocational education and enhancing the global governance of vocational education.

2. Proactively Serving International Collaboration in Industrial Capacity

As global collaboration of industrial and supply chain deepens, the unique connection between vocational education and industry has gained increasing attention. We should continue to promote the establishment of an international cooperation mechanism for vocational education that highlights "industry-education integration and school-enterprise collaboration." We should also continue to co-build "small yet impactful" livelihood projects in the educational field, such as "Luban Workshop," foster new growth points in cooperation, and assist the world in industrial upgrades and green, sustainable development via vocational education while promoting international collaboration in industrial capacity, helping partner countries train skilled talents and create high-quality employment opportunities.

3. Promoting the Establishment of an International Framework for Vocational Education Standards

Standards represent the collective achievements of human civilizations and facilitate the interconnectivity among countries worldwide. We should look into creating a cooperative framework that involves multiple countries, aiming to find the greatest common interests among all parties engaged in multilateral cooperation. Additionally, we should develop a vocational educational and training framework that aligns with the future demands for professional skills. These efforts will promote the mutual recognition of skills and qualifications across countries, creating a stable, unified, and regulated global vocational education environment and promoting high-quality development of vocational education worldwide.

Chapter Four: Primary Measures

2024 marks the onset of China's initiative to establish itself as a leading education power. Vocational education closely follows national strategic objectives, driven by a steadfast commitment and actionable measures under the principle of "genuinely enhancing vocational education." Relevant action plan has been implemented to accelerate the development of a vocational education system that effectively integrates vocational and general education and promotes collaboration between industry and education.

I. Enhancing the Mechanism for Integrating Vocational and General Education

1. Enriching Means and Pathways for Vocational Enlightenment Education

We will develop a systematic curriculum and a practical teaching system specifically tailored to the developmental characteristics of youth. Vocational schools are encouraged to deliver courses, provide vocational lectures, customize classes, and facilitate paired mentorships at regular schools. These initiatives should be designed to implement vocational enlightenment education, labor education, vocational experiences, and skill-based courses within regular elementary and secondary schools. In addition, these schools are also encouraged to operate exchange events, such as inviting model craftsmen and outstanding vocational students to share their experiences on campuses. Moreover, a group of vocational schools will open vocational enlightenment education and labor education bases within their campuses, specifically serving elementary and secondary students.

2. Expanding Channels for Student Development, both Vertically and Horizontally

Pilot projects will be implemented to create more diverse high schools, such as comprehensive high schools. These pilot projects aim to promote the mutual sharing of teaching staff and selectable courses, the mutual transfer of student records, and the mutual recognition of credits between secondary vocational schools and general high schools. Provinces are encouraged to implement integrated training programs, such as the 5-year (3+2) secondary to higher vocational program, the 7-year (3+4) secondary to higher bachelor's/applied bachelor's degree vocational program, and the 5-year (3+2) higher associate degree to higher bachelor's/applied bachelor's degree vocational program. Provinces are also encouraged to standardize this training model to help students' transition from high-quality secondary vocational schools to higher vocational schools or application-oriented universities. In addition, initiatives have been introduced to encourage graduates from regular bachelor's degree programs to pursue vocational education and ultimately find skill-based employment. These new models and paths for lifelong vocational training are being actively explored.

3. Optimizing the Vocational Education Evaluation Systems, the Entrance Examination for Vocational Schools in particular

We will refine the examination and enrollment systems to align with the school-running principles of vocational education and the growth patterns of skilled talent. This involves perfecting the admission process that combines "Cultural Literacy + Vocational Skills." Provinces will be supported in tailoring their own "Entrance Examination for Vocational Schools" schemes according to local conditions, further improving the content and format of these exams to provide students with diversified pathways for growth and success. Additionally, support will be extended to the national "Double High-Level Plan," which aims to elevate outstanding higher vocational colleges to vocational undergraduate schools. Application-oriented universities are encouraged to set up vocational undergraduate majors. There will also be a steady increase in the enrollment quota for application-oriented universities and vocational undergraduate schools in the "Entrance Examination for Vocational Schools."

II. Enhancing the Mechanism to Align Vocational Education with Economic and Industrial Development

1. Strengthening Provincial Vocational Education Systems

The Ministry of Education and provincial governments will deepen their collaborative mechanisms to advance vocational education, urging provincial governments to draft lists detailing industrial development, talent needs, and policy support tailored to their specific regional contexts. These lists will serve as targeted projects and platforms to propel vocational education reforms. A digital mapping system will be established to align local vocational education resources with industrial layouts, guiding vocational schools in their industry-education integration practices to identify their directions and maximize their impact. Construction of vocational schools at all levels will be strengthened by granting them autonomy in internal organization, job positioning, personnel planning, teacher recruitment, and professional title review processes. Increased funding for vocational education will establish a long-term incentive mechanism for skill-oriented talent, ensuring the effective supply of human resources.

2. Strengthening Municipal Industry-Education Integration Communities

Centering on the needs of areas with economic factors and industrial development functions, such as the nation's seven major regional development strategies, 19 national-level new areas, 178 national high-tech industrial development zones, 229 national economic development zones, and 17 national airport economic demonstration zones—local governments are encouraged to create plans and policies that mobilize in-depth cooperation among governments, industrial enterprises, and research institutions in co-designing curricula, co-creating talent training programs, co-developing courses and textbooks, and co-building faculty with vocational schools. Schools are guided to closely align with local industrial structures and market employment demands by optimizing their majors and collaborating with industrial enterprises on technical challenges, providing technical consultation and services to businesses in parks, thus fostering technological innovation and product upgrades. Local authorities will be driven to strengthen municipal industry-education integration communities, expanding vocational education resources from economically developed regions to counties (cities).

3. Strengthening Sector-Specific Industry-Education Integration Communities

Around key sectors such as advanced manufacturing, modern agriculture, and modern services, there will be continued efforts to build sector-specific industry-education integration communities that are large in scale, systemic, and institutionalized. These communities will leverage industrial chains to synchronize industry and educational resources across different regions, enhance communication and cooperation among enterprises along the supply chain, and tailor talent recruitment to the specific needs of the industry in terms of type, level, and structure. Schools and businesses within these communities will implement joint enrollment programs and cultivate the needed industry talent through entrusted training, orders, and apprenticeships. Support will be provided for the integration of school and enterprise resources to construct public training bases for practical skills, highly skilled talents, and vocational skill training, making lifelong vocational training viable.

4. Optimizing Resource Allocation at High-Level Vocational Schools

A new set of national demonstration and guidance projects will be launched to establish a network of top-tier vocational schools and clusters of majors. These initiatives will focus on serving local industries, regional strategies, and the "One Body, Two Wings" initiative. Additionally, they also aim to improve people's quality of life, promote vocational education going abroad, and advance international collaboration in vocational education. Effective use of evaluation as a guiding tool will optimize the overall design of resource allocation, evaluation methods, and assessment mechanisms at vocational schools, steering them from "good foundation, good conditions" toward "good service, good support."

III. Advancing of "New Infrastructure" at Vocational Schools Steadfastly

1. Developing High-Level Majors Matching Demand and Concentrating Elements

We will thoroughly analyze the actual demands for skilled talents across various segments and positions for key national industrial chains such as advanced manufacturing and digital industry clusters. The analysis will guide vocational schools in establishing new majors relevant to the real economy and emerging sectors in short supply while phasing out outdated and oversupplied majors. In addition, it will also guide vocational schools to enhance traditional majors through digital upgrades and transformations and promote the cluster-based development of majors to cultivate highly skilled talents who are versatile, innovative, and growth-oriented. Vocational schools with the right conditions are encouraged to offer training in vital livelihood areas such as childcare, nursing, health and wellness, and domestic services to meet the needs of accessible childcare, community-embedded nursing, and community-based elder care, among other new institutions.

2. Creating First-Class Core Courses Matching Real Positions and Integrated with Digital Intelligence

Vocational schools are encouraged to deeply engage with industry and enterprise production lines to conduct research on the skill requirements for talents and vocational positions. This will advance the reform of core courses with the most immediate connection to key vocational skills and the greatest impact on the training of highly skilled talents. The construction of key projects such as teaching resource databases for vocational majors, national online excellent courses, first-class core courses, and virtual simulation training bases should be promoted. The aim is to create more scenario-based classrooms and leverage digital and smart technologies to drive the transformation of educational methods and assessment approaches.

3. Developing High-Quality Industry-Education Integration Textbooks with Diverse Contributors and Formats

Based on the spectrum of capabilities, leading companies, high-level vocational schools, and industry experts are organized to co-author a diverse array of high-quality textbooks that reflect cutting-edge industry technologies. Real companies' production processes and technical standards will be promptly transformed into textbook content, with typical tasks and production orders selected from high-quality enterprise training materials. Efforts to develop digital textbooks will intensify, leading to breakthroughs in the creation of digital textbooks. China is actively promoting loose-leaf and workbook-style textbooks while encouraging the utilization of nationally planned textbooks and other high-quality materials.

4. Cultivating Well-Structured and Highly Skilled Teams of "Double-Qualified" Teachers

We will perfect the system for the training and practice of high-level vocational education teachers, relying on leading companies and high-level higher education institutions to establish national training bases for "Double-Qualified" teachers. Targeting young teachers, integrated industry-study-research training and on-the-job practice programs will be offered. Moreover, we will take in-depth action to enhance the academic qualifications of vocational school teachers and thoroughly implement the New Era Vocational School Famous Teachers (Craftsmen) and Principals Training Program to nurture an outstanding teacher team. Vocational school teachers and highly skilled professionals are encouraged to take on each other's roles part-time within the framework of regulations. The guarantee system for performance-based pay for vocational school teachers will be improved. Training in digital teaching skills will be enhanced to boost teachers' awareness, ability, and sense of responsibility in utilizing digital technology to optimize, innovate, and transform educational activities.

5. Establishing High-Level Vocational Training Bases with Realistic Scenarios and Open Integration

In line with the latest trends in industrial development and real-world production scenarios, vocational schools are encouraged to set up open regional industry-education integrated practice centers. These centers will blend practical teaching, social training, real production, and technical services. In addition, various public practice centers and enterprise practice centers are needed to help promote the digital and intelligent upgrade of vocational school training bases. The student internship and practice system also needs improvement, focusing on developing a series of typical production practice projects that can be applied in actual enterprise production sites, regional industry-education integrated practice centers, or on-campus productive training bases. This approach will enhance students' hands-on operation skills, facilitate the transformation of technological achievements into productivity, and foster scientific innovation.

IV. Strengthening Equal Emphasis on Training and Education

1. Deepening Training for Industrial Technicians

It is crucial to enhance both academic education and non-academic training for industrial technicians. The initiative "Fulfilling Dreams of Pursuing Education" for industrial workers will be fully implemented. We will improve the entrance examination system for higher vocational schools and promote the Chinese-style apprenticeship model to help industrial workers achieve higher education through parttime study and work. We will initiate knowledge-updating projects for professional technicians by effectively utilizing open regional industry-education integrated practice centers, public training bases, and highly skilled talent training bases. The vocational training action plan will be fully implemented to promote employment and entrepreneurship, with extensive pre-employment digital skills training, on-the-job training, and job transition training available to enhance the digital skills of industrial technicians.

2. Deepening Training for New Professional Farmers

We will enhance coordination among municipal governments to manage vocational education centers at the county level effectively. This involves integrating vocational skills training projects and funding while actively supporting the establishment of agriculture-related vocational education majors. The aim is to create a cluster of majors that precisely supports the goal of rural revitalization. In addition, we will implement a targeted scheme for admission, training, and employment to achieve the vision of "One College Graduate per Village." Moreover, we will conduct extensive training for rural labor transfer, practical rural technology training, and capacity-building initiatives for rural community leaders. These efforts are designed to accelerate the development of rural experts in science and technology and cultivate growth leaders, ultimately supporting rural revitalization through talent and skills.

3. Deepening Training for Community Residents

We will create community learning centers at the county level, designed to provide a comprehensive and accessible lifelong education system along with a robust institutional framework, making our vision of the "15-Minute Learning Circle" a reality. By combining online and offline learning formats—such as micro-lessons, community lectures, and evening classes for residents—we aim to offer community members valuable experiences in practical skills useful in both work and daily life, as well as public skill development services. Additionally, we will enhance the establishment of community colleges specifically for the elderly, fostering a network for resource sharing and collaborative development. We will create engaging courses tailored for seniors while also offering the wider community access to classes in culture and creativity, intangible cultural heritage, traditional handicrafts, vocational training, life skills, and hobbies.

V. Advancing the Digitalization of Vocational Education

1. Upgrading the National Platform of Smart Education for Vocational Education

We plan to deeply integrate smart technology into vocational education teaching, enhancing and refining the platform's functionality to provide full-coverage, personalized services for students, teachers, and education administrators alike. For intelligence-assisted learning, we will create smart learning partners and tutors while exploring 24/7 online Q&A through AI customer service, delivering learners with one-step, full-process support throughout their learning journey. Regarding intelligence-assisted teaching, we will develop intelligent teaching assistants that will aid teachers in lesson preparation, lighten their workload, and boost their efficiency, enabling them to focus more on creative teaching activities. In the realm of intelligence-assisted administration, we will create smart homework systems, interactive classrooms, online teaching research, assisted grading, evaluation, and various other digital tools and platforms.

2. Developing and Compiling High-Quality Digital Learning Resources

We will employ a mix of approaches like teacher-student co-creation, autonomous school development, and government-coordinated planning to enhance resources for specialized courses, arts education, and labor education. We will continuously improve key projects, such as teaching resource databases for vocational majors and high-quality online open courses, to expand the availability of vocational education resources. At the same time, we will focus on creating digital textbooks and collecting various teaching aids, lesson plans, courseware, teaching plan designs, and virtual simulation training resources to diversify vocational education resources. Additionally, we will innovate our resource evaluation methods by leveraging dynamic data collected from the National Education Big Data Center to assess platform resources' scale, structure, content, and effectiveness, thus supporting the full-life cycle management of vocational education resources, spanning their development, entry, updating, and removal.

3. Implementing Large-Scale Digital Application Demonstrations in Vocational Education

We will actively push for the application of the National Platform of Smart Education for Vocational Education in all regions and for individuals at every stage of the process, expanding the reach of high-quality resources and advancing our initiatives from pilot programs to demonstration projects. Vocational schools are encouraged to integrate the platform's resources and smart services into their teaching practices, utilizing digital educational resources to enrich students' extracurricular activities while supporting their interests and hobbies. Furthermore, we aim to enhance the development of smart campuses within vocational schools, actively adapting to evolving learning methods and exploring the extensive use of digital tools to empower personalized learning, innovative teaching, and individualized education. We will also refine international versions of the National Platform of Smart Education for Vocational Education to provide better services tailored to diverse regions, countries, and languages.

VI. Facilitating High-Level International Exchanges and Cooperation

1. Establishing a More Resilient Platform for Global Vocational Education Exchanges

We are committed to develop platforms such as the China-ASEAN Vocational Education Exhibition and Forum, the China-Eurasia Expo-International Forum on Education, the Future of Africa-Vocational Education Cooperation Plan, and the BRICS Technical and Vocational Education and Training (TVET) Cooperation Alliance while enhancing the mechanisms for international exchange and collaboration in vocational education. Moreover, we will continue to establish international vocational education alliances, set up international vocational education awards, and organize exhibitions for vocational and technical education as we continue to host the World Vocational and Technical Education Development Conference to the highest standards.

2. Making the Vocational School Skills Competitions More International

We will continue to optimize the World Vocational College Skills Competition by improving the design of competition tracks and refining its content and format to better meet the actual needs of production, management, and service frontlines. The competition will be structured to thoroughly evaluate students' abilities and skills, incorporating new categories based on recent global trends to broaden its scope. Furthermore, we will strengthen our communication and collaboration with international vocational education organizations and the organizer of WorldSkills Competition.

3. Shaping Brands for International Exchanges in Vocational Education

We will further enhance the international collaboration skills of vocational schools. By establishing training bases that follow the "Chinese Language + Vocational Skills" model, we aim to train international talents and develop skilled local personnel that Chinese-funded enterprises urgently need. Our efforts will also include advancing branded projects like the Luban Workshop, Silk Road School, and the Center for Chinese Language and Professional Skills. These initiatives will enable us to promote international cooperation via industry-education integration and school-enterprise collaborations, optimizing project operations, project entry processes, and the mechanisms for quality monitoring and exit.

4. Co-Creating and Sharing Vocational Education Standards

We encourage vocational schools to rely on currently operating international vocational education cooperation projects to join industrial enterprises in developing robust vocational teaching standards, curriculum standards, and internship and practical training standards that are industry-leading and globally recognized, as well as in promoting their implementation in vocational schools both domestically and internationally.

郑重声明

高等教育出版社依法对本书享有专有出版权。任何未经许可的复制、销售行为均违反《中华人民共和国著作权法》，其行为人将承担相应的民事责任和行政责任；构成犯罪的，将被依法追究刑事责任。为了维护市场秩序，保护读者的合法权益，避免读者误用盗版书造成不良后果，我社将配合行政执法部门和司法机关对违法犯罪的单位和个人进行严厉打击。社会各界人士如发现上述侵权行为，希望及时举报，我社将奖励举报有功人员。

反盗版举报电话 （010）58581999 58582371

反盗版举报邮箱 dd@hep.com.cn

通信地址 北京市西城区德外大街 4 号
         高等教育出版社知识产权与法律事务部

邮政编码 100120

读者意见反馈

为收集对教材的意见建议，进一步完善教材编写并做好服务工作，读者可将对本教材的意见建议通过如下渠道反馈至我社。

咨询电话 400-810-0598

反馈邮箱 zz_dzyj@pub.hep.cn

通信地址 北京市朝阳区惠新东街 4 号富盛大厦 1 座
         高等教育出版社总编辑办公室

邮政编码 100029